Henry Moore Teller

The Fisheries Treaty

Speech of Hon. Henry M. Teller, of Colorado

Henry Moore Teller

The Fisheries Treaty
Speech of Hon. Henry M. Teller, of Colorado

ISBN/EAN: 9783337155582

Printed in Europe, USA, Canada, Australia, Japan

Cover: Foto ©ninafisch / pixelio.de

More available books at **www.hansebooks.com**

THE FISHERIES TREATY.

SPEECH

OF

Hon. HENRY M. TELLER,

OF COLORADO,

IN THE

SENATE OF THE UNITED STATES,

JULY 21, 1888.

WASHINGTON.
1888.

The Fisheries Treaty.

SPEECH

OF

HON. HENRY M. TELLER.

The Senate having under consideration the fisheries treaty in open executive session—

Mr. TELLER said:

Mr. PRESIDENT: I congratulate the Senate and I congratulate the country that we approach the discussion of this case from what I consider a proper business standpoint; that we are discussing this question in the presence of the whole American people; that we, the agents of the people, are giving our reasons for and against this treaty, the reasons that shall govern our votes, in their hearing, and in so doing we are recognizing our obligation to them.

The Senators who have favored this treaty have, without exception I believe in this discussion, alluded to the fact that we had taken, or were taking, into our councils not only the American people, but all the people of Great Britain interested in this subject, and the Senators who have favored by their speeches in this Chamber the ratification of this treaty have been pronounced in their opinion that such discussion in open session was contrary to the great interests of the American people. They have put it, I suppose, on the ground that we are notifying the English Government of the weakness of our case. The President of the United States notified the people of Great Britain of the weakness of our case in his message to the Senate. The Secretary of State, in his communication to the President and in his public utterances made from time to time, either by letter or in public speeches, or in interviews through the newspapers, has given the English-speaking people of the world to understand that this treaty is more than we are entitled to under the convention of 1818. Sir, when the English people and the American people shall attempt to negotiate another convention, they will not refer to the speeches made in this Chamber in support of the proposition that the offers made in this treaty are all that we are entitled to and more, but they will recur to the official language of the Executive of the nation, to the official language of the Secretary of State; and it is folly to say that this treaty can not be discussed in the open Senate by the American Senate for fear that our utterances will be used against this Government hereafter when the Executive and the Department of the Government charged with this branch of the public service have been so free with their utterances, both official and otherwise.

I notice, I think, that every Senator who approaches this subject from the other side has declared his objection to its discussion in public. I notice also that every Senator who has approached the subject from that side at least has declared that inasmuch as the discussion was to be in open Senate it should be free and it should be full, and that so far as he was concerned there should be no withholding from the public and from the world the views that were entertained of this subject; and yet when we have got these declarations of the several Senators who have addressed the Senate we have discovered nothing that might not have been proclaimed from the housetops. We have heard nothing that the President had'not already said; we have heard nothing that the Secretary of State had not said; we have heard nothing that had not been said by the public press of the Democratic party in defense of this treaty.

So, Mr. President, after all, while I admit that this case is *sui generis*, while I admit that it does not stand in its relations to a public discussion on the same basis with some of the treaties we make, while I admit that there are reasons for the public discussion of this treaty that do not exist as to all others, I think it may be said that this instance has demonstrated at least that no danger will come to the Republic by an open discussion of a treaty in the United States Senate in the presence of the sixty-odd millions of American people. It has been discussed in Great Britain; it has been discussed in Canada; it has been ratified, I understand, by the Canadian government, ratified and approved by the British Government.

I believe I will mention the fact, as my attention is called to it by the Senator from Vermont who sits in front of me [Mr. EDMUNDS], that it had the unanimous approval when the vote was taken of the Canadian Parliament. I have not been informed and am not able to state because I do not know and have not heard of any objection to this treaty that was made in the British Parliament.

The Senator who first addressed the Senate on this subject on the other side'was free to talk about the influence of caucus. He told us that there was a caucus combination to bring the Senate first to reject the treaty and then to consider it in open session. Now, I venture to say that neither the Senator from Alabama [Mr. MORGAN] nor any other Senator can point to a Senator on this side of the Chamber who has ever at any time given any intimation that he proposed to support this treaty; and inasmuch as this question of caucus domination and caucus control has been freely discussed by at least three Senators on the other side, I propose to say that that point was never discussed in our caucus. The Republican party, indeed, were against this treaty from its very first publication.

I may say more, that a great many Senators sitting on the other side of the Chamber were likewise against it at its first publication. The Republican Senators, I say, without exception were against it, and a very respectable number of the Senators on the other side were against it.

I understand that the Senators on the other side also caucused about this matter. They caucused as to whether they would discuss it in open session, and I believe a very considerable number of them advocated in caucus and voted in caucus—as we were told by a Democratic Senator in executive session, the proceedings of which have been made public, and of which I have a right to speak—in favor of its discussion in the open Senate.

A Senator in my hearing suggests that it is safe to say that two-thirds of the American Senate were opposed to this treaty. Mr. President, I said in executive session, and I repeat it here, that if this treaty had come from a Republican administration I do not believe there is a Republican on this side of the Chamber who would have supported it, and I know that there is not a Democrat on that side of the Chamber who would have supported it if it had not come from a Democratic administration; and I know more than that, that there is not any considerable number of Senators on that side of the Chamber who would have supported this treaty but for the fact that the power of the Administration was brought upon that body to compel support of this treaty.

If any Senator desires proof that the Administration is the active propagandist of this treaty, I will furnish it. If not, I think I can rest upon the general assertion. Surely when you see the Secretary of State writing letters for publication, when you see the members of this commission, who were connected with the Administration, making public addresses in its defense and support, when you find the Secretary of State submitting to newspaper interviews in order that he may give the public his views of this treaty, I do not need to go to further proof to show that the whole force of this Administration has been brought to bear to compel the Democratic Senators and the Democratic party to accept this as a Democratic measure.

The Senator from Alabama [Mr. MORGAN] attempted to give a history of the way in which this treaty came into open session. Now, I may say in the presence of my fellow-Senators of my side, that I was perhaps as active as any man on our side in bringing this question before the open Senate, and I think I am not mistaken as to how this matter stood. The Senator from Alabama said, as I recollect, that there had been originally forty-one votes in favor of its discussion in secret, and three only in favor of its discussion in the open Senate, the three consisting of the Senator who sits on my left, from Massachusetts [Mr. DAWES], the Senator from Ohio [Mr. SHERMAN], and myself. No member of the Senate has forgotten that when that propo..tion came before the Senate in secret session the Senator from Alabama declared in substance that if this treaty was to be attacked by the Republican Senators as a treaty as a whole, without amendment, he was in favor of its discussion in open Senate. I would say that there were several Senators, including the Senator from Connecticut [Mr. PLATT], the Senator from Virginia [Mr. RIDDLEBERGER], the Senator from Oregon [Mr. MITCHELL], and others, who had always voted in favor of open sessions who were not here when that vote was taken. I will say further that when the Republican caucus voted upon this question there were only three men in it who voted against the open discussion of this treaty.

I know that several of the Senators put it upon the ground that the case was sui generis. I know several of them reserved for themselves the right to insist that this was not a precedent binding on them in the future. But upon this question we were practically unanimous. The Senator knows very well, as do all the Senators who were in that executive session, that that vote was not a test whether this treaty should be discussed in open session or not. He knows very well that the Democratic side of the Senate were presented to us in the attitude of being ready to go into open executive session if we did not propose to amend the treaty. He knows it was said then and there by a number of Senators on this side that the treaty was of such a character that no amendment could be properly made to it. I myself saying in executive session that it was a treaty unfit to be amended, and incapable of being amended to be consistent and harmonious with the purpose and object declared by the State Department. So, Mr. President, the Republican Senators are not in condition to be criticised or castigated on this account.

Then came later the vote in executive session by which practically the whole matter was decided by the Senator from Maine [Mr. HALE]. When that vote was taken, at least six men on the other side of the Chamber voted with us for an open session. When they saw that the Republicans meant open session (which they did not believe before), then these six withdrew their votes before the result was announced. Included in that number are some of the Senators who are to-day criticising us for discussing this question in open Senate.

So, Mr. President, we are here to discuss this question as I believe all questions of this kind ought to be discussed, where we can face the sentiment of the American people; and since the discussion has begun I believe there has been practically but one sentiment in the country upon this treaty. Although the attempt has been made by the Administration to commit the Democratic party to it, it has met with very little success, for with the exception perhaps of a few persons in certain sections, there has been no interest in its ratification expressed by anybody.

The question of our fishery rights on the northern coast is not a small question, and it is not a local question. The people of Colorado who never avail themselves of these rights have as much interest in them in one sense as the people of Maine, Massachusetts, or any of the New England States. So far as they concern our honor, our dignity, and our rights they have the same interest in them as any other citizens can have, although they may have a pecuniary benefit in the use of the property belonging to the United States, for that is what this fishery claim is.

We in the Western country would not be willing that the United States should part with its rights and its privileges because we receive no pecuniary benefit. because we can not start out fishing smacks and fishing fleets. If the fishery is a right that belongs to the people of the United States we want it maintained, and we are in favor of its maintenance. as we are in favor of maintaining every other right.

We recognize the fact that when the treaty of 1783 was made there were three things that stood out paramount in that treaty. First, our independen ; second, the establishment of our boundaries; and third, and not le : closely connected therewith, our fishery rights; and we should as quickly think of surrendering a portion of the State of Maine at the dictation or the bidding of British greed as we would think of surrendering a single foot of fishing ground that properly belongs to the nation. And I am glad to say that we do not belong to the class of men who purchase peace by the surrender of that which is unquestionably ours. Willing always as we are, as are all the American people, to concede questions of doubtful authority, of a doubtful character, we are never to be intimidated by threats of war or suggestions of difficulties that will be incurred in the maintenance of that which we all agree rightfully belongs to us.

Mr. President, Great Britain might call upon us to surrender a piece of Maine that would be so small and so worthless as to be insignificant in comparison with the great cost it would be to us to insist upon our rights by war, and yet is there anywhere in this country a citizen so mean and of so little spirit that he would surrender an acre of the rocks of New England at the demand of Great Britain or of all the world? And if so, why should we surrender that which is of equal value and the surrender of which would be equal degradation and disgrace?

Mr. President, we came to these fishery rights exactly as we came to our boundary rights, exactly as we came to our territorial boundaries, exactly as we came to our independence. It has been said again and again that there is not a rod of that country that our ancestors had not fought for. If Great Britain succeeded in dominating that northern sea and compelling her great rival of that time to yield to her it was because the American fisherman made it possible, and made it possible too when British love of peace was in favor of its surrender.

If there is a great British dominion growing up upon our Northern border, it is because the New England fishermen, prior to the Revolution, made it possible for Great Britain to build and rear this great political structure on our north. And so, when our ancestors came to this question, they did not say to Britain, "We want you should give us this;" they said, "It is ours of right;" and from that day to this there has never been anybody until it has been heard in this Senate—and that, too, within the last two months—who has denied our right. The right of Great Britain has been uniformly considered exactly as that of a copartner, a cotenant, the United States and Great Britain being owners in common. These terms have all been used again and again by American authorities in the defense of our rights. Nay, they have never been denied. No English authority has ever questioned our rights as equal in all respects except as we surrendered them by the treaty of 1818, and what we did not there surrender is ours to this day as much as it ever was, not by virtue of a treaty any more than our independence is conceded by virtue of a treaty, not any more by treaty than the boundaries fixed between Great Britain's dominion on this continent and ours were fixed by treaty.

In 1818 we modified the treaty of 1783. We surrendered some things that were ours, but, as the Senator from Massachusetts [Mr. HOAR] showed, not without consideration in return. We gave up some things and we got others that were considered then an equivalent. It was not, as has been said, a surrender; it was not a yielding, for the American people at that time were not in the habit of surrendering that which belonged to them. They had gone to war with Great Britain for the purpose of denying a right that the British asserted, the right of search by sea; and when the war was over, and when this question came to be settled, our people insisted that we were, so far as the fisheries were concerned, as we had been before, and when the negotiations were going on for the subsequent treaty it was everywhere insisted in the United States that we would not surrender an inch of territory, nor would we surrender a single privilege that was ours under the treaty of 1783.

Nobody who has studied this question can forget the letter of Mr. Adams which he wrote to Mr. Madison, in which he said that he would continue the war forever before he would surrender the fisheries. We never did surrender. We exchanged with the British for what privileges we did not have under the treaty of 1783; we took some that we did not have, and we gave up some that we did have. And from that time up to 1830, a period of twelve years, there does not appear anywhere in history that I can find an instance where our rights were questioned or doubted to be exactly what we insist now they are. Practically they were never disputed until 1841 by any authority that was worthy of attention, and practically I might say not seriously until 1843.

Contemporaneous exposition, then, of the treaty of 1818 is on the American side; it is according to our view—a view that has been maintained by everybody connected with this question. Notwithstanding the assertion that the great Secretary of State, Daniel Webster, gave away our case, notwithstanding the assertion made in this Chamber that Edward Everett gave away this case, I assert here without fear of successful contradiction that nothing of the kind can be found, that every act of every administration, from the day the convention of 1818 was ratified up to the time that this treaty was signed, had been in favor of the American idea and the American construction of the treaty of 1818.

Mr. President, in 1841, or perhaps in 1839, one of the British provinces made claim of a character inconsistent with the construction put upon the treaty by the American Government, a claim which practically appears to have slept until about 1843. I do not intend to go into the general headland theory. I do not intend to discuss the question of bays with the Senator from Delaware [Mr. GRAY], whom I do not see present. It is enough for me to know that all of the public authorities in this country have uniformly held one way upon this subject, and it is enough for me to know that Great Britain, the real and respectable party in the case, had acquiesced in that, and had abandoned practically any claim set up either under the headland theory or the broad-bay theory.

Senators who have preceded me have spoken of the Argus and the Washington cases as having thoroughly and completely established our position. I know the Senator from Delaware who addressed the Senate some time since on this subject insisted that the case of the Washington did not settle anything; and yet the British Government acquiesced in that as a determination not only whether we had a right to fish in the Bay of Fundy, but in all other bays of like character and similarly situated. And if there is any headland theory to-day in existence in the minds of the British authorities, it is because this Administration has revived it; it is because this Administration has brought out from the old rubbish of the past this exploded theory that the right existed to include as British ground all the sea that was within a line drawn from headland to headland, no matter how long it might be or how great. But the American Senate and the American people are not likely to accept this new discovery of this Administration, and are not likely to avail themselves of this old and exploded theory.

Mr. President, from 1843, the time of the decision in the Washington case, down to 1852 there was practical quiet over this disputed question. In 1852 the British Government sent several armed vessels to the northern seas where these issues were liable to arise. In 1850, before this was done, we had overtures from the British Government for reciprocity with Canada. Our people had not taken kindly to the idea, and it was thought perhaps then, as seems to be thought now, that a little coercion would be valuable; that a little pressure might be brought upon us to compel us to yield to their demand, and so a British fleet was sent there with orders to look out for the American fishermen.

The matter came into the American Senate, and I wish to call the attention of the Senate very briefly to some observations then made. The discussion was participated in by the most prominent and leading men of that day, notably by Mr. Rusk, of Texas; Mr. Borland, of Arkansas; Mr. Davis, of Massachusetts; Mr. Toucey, of Connecticut; Mr. Mason, of Virginia; Mr. Hamlin, of Maine; Mr. Cass, of Michigan; Mr. Soulé, of Louisiana, and a great many others.

It was asserted then that some of these vessels had been sent into the

Canadian waters for the purpose of intimidating the Government of the United States into the execution of a reciprocity treaty. It is somewhat interesting to compare now with then the utterances of the principal and leading Democrats of this body. To-day I find, so far as there has been any discussion of this question on the Democratic side, every Democratic Senator who has arisen has presented the extreme British view of the case. Every worn-out and exploded theory, every fallacious argument, every absurdity that has been put forth by Canada and repudiated by Great Britain finds its advocates on this floor. And I confess myself to some degree of humiliation when I hear a statement made by a Senator of the United States as to the rights of this Government that is in perfect antagonism to that which has been declared by every Secretary of State who has ever passed upon the question, the present Secretary of State included; and my disgust, if I may use the term properly in this body, is not modified by the fact that each Senator, as he thus advocates British doctrine and the British side of the question, declares with his hand upon his breast that he is actuated and influenced only by the highest patriotism while his opponents are influenced and actuated by only the basest partisan purposes.

Oh, Mr. President, the Democratic party here and elsewhere will not be able to make the American people believe that the long line of honorable men who have been heard upon this question, and who have stood here and advocated the doctrine that we advocate as to the construction of the treaty of 1818, were actuated solely by partisan purposes. Let them explain why it is that they have within a twelve-month changed their position on this subject, and in so doing are actuated by only high and patriotic resolves.

Now, Mr. President, I will submit without reading all of them some of the remarks made in the Senate in 1852. I wish it would not encumber the RECORD too much to put in all that Lewis Cass said in a speech of great length on this subject. No Democrat rose in the Senate in 1852 to defend the British Government, to apologize for its outrages, or to defend its construction of the treaty of 1818. Nay, more; there was no man of any political faith who did that. It was left for the later day and for the Administration of Grover Cleveland to find men willing to stand here and assert that all their predecessors had been wrong and that we had always been in the wrong and the British Government and the Canadian provinces in their claims had been in the right.

Mr. Borland, of Arkansas, in 1852, said:

It is a remarkable fact that in looking back through the history of our Government, especially to the war period of 1812, and since that time in every dispute or hostile collision with a foreign country, without an exception that now occurs to me, there has been a party in our country and represented in the two Houses of Congress which has invariably taken sides with that foreign country and against our own.—*Hon. Solon Borland* (Arkansas), July 23, 1852.

Yet, notwithstanding that assertion, I repeat that an examination of the records will show that nobody asserted on this floor, nobody asserted in any branch of the Government that the British construction was right. With one accord those men asserted that it was beneath the dignity of the United States to treat with Great Britain while Great Britain had a hostile fleet on our borders, and with one united voice they declared that it was the duty of the Government of the United States to put in those seas gun for gun and ship for ship. We may be excused to-day from making that assertion or that claim. We can not well do it, and we can not do it because the votes on the other side of the Chamber and the Democratic party as represented in the other branch of Congress for years have rendered it impossible for us so to do.

I now ask to have these extracts from that debate inserted without reading.

DEBATE OF 1852.

The conduct of Great Britain in this business should be met promptly on our side. It is supposed by some Senators to be designed to bring about an enactment for reciprocity of trade on our part with the British colonies. If that be so I will never give a vote for such a measure under such circumstances, no matter what may be the consequences. I will never yield to any threats made by the British Government.

It is said upon the other hand that it is for the purpose of bringing about a negotiation by which the British Government will acquire rights in another quarter similar to those which they have acceded to us on the northern coast, and which we claim there. Sir, is this the way to negotiate?

It is due to ourselves to protect our rights. I would do nothing to bring on war, but I would not submit to this domineering spirit which has manifested itself too much in all the conduct of Great Britain with other nations.—*Hon. Thomas J. Rusk* (Texas), July 23.

It may be true that the proposition for reciprocal trade between the British colonies and the United States is at the bottom of this. But I ask if such a course as has been pursued is the way to open negotiations with us? Has it ever happened before in the whole history of our country, from the day when our independence was acknowledged by Great Britain until this administration, that negotiations have been opened with us through the medium of cannon pointed against our citizens and our ships? If there be such an instance in our history, I confess my ignorance of it, and I would gladly have remained in ignorance to my dying day that such a thing could be.—*Hon. Solon Borland* (Arkansas), July 23.

I do not believe that in all the great interests of the country there is one that merits protection more. From that nursery springs the great body of navigators and men of enterprise who adorn and embellish the country. If you take away that protecting arm of the Government you take that which is more essential in you in the defense of the country than any other thing that can be named. The enterprise, the skill, and the courage of these men are manifest as far as our name and fame extend. * * * This is the nursery of the skill and strength which are indispensable to success on the ocean.—*Hon. John Davis* (Massachusetts), July 23.

I concur most fully in the sentiments of the Senator from Massachusetts, with regard to the magnitude of the fishing industry. It has ever been cherished by the Government and the people of this country, as one of the very highest importance, not only as a profitable employment, but as a nursery for seamen. I feel confident that nothing which has been said, or that will be said in this Senate, will operate adversely to that interest. I must say, however, that if it be proposed to open now a negotiation on that subject under the mouths of British cannon, it is a mode of initiating it that does not commend itself to my judgment as a citizen of this country, or as a member of this Senate. I trust, sir, that no Government of this country will ever open a negotiation in regard to any interest in this exceptionable, and, I may say, humiliating manner.—*Hon. Isaac Toucey* (Connecticut), July 23.

I know not what these regulations are, but if it means anything it means that we are to negotiate under duress. Aye, sir, at this day that this great people, covering a continent and numbering five and twenty millions, are to negotiate with a foreign fleet on our coast. I know not what the President has done; I claim to know what the American people expect of him. I know that if he has done his duty his reply will be, "I have ordered the whole naval force of the country into those seas to protect the rights of American fishermen against British cannon."—*Hon. James M. Mason* (Virginia), July 23.

We shall need these men hereafter; we shall need them, as we have needed them, to fight our battles upon the ocean and upon the lakes. * * * When that time shall come it is the American fisherman who will fight your battles, as he fought them in the war of 1812. Then, when the British Government threatened to sweep our little but gallant Navy from the ocean and to annihilate our commerce, it was the fishermen from Marblehead and all along our coast who rallied with patriotic hearts and with ready hands to sustain the Stars and Stripes of our country; and it was by their prowess that Great Britain was made to feel the force of a freeman's arm whenever wielded in a holy cause. Whenever the cross of St. George went down before the Stars and Stripes we were indebted mainly to them for that victory. We shall be faithless to the trust that has been reposed in us if we do not sustain and stand by what are their legal, their international, and their treaty rights. Stand by them, as they have always stood by their country. They ask no more.—*Hon. Hannibal Hamlin* (Maine), August 5.

We did not get the right to fish on the ocean from England or any other earthly power. We got it from Almighty God, and we mean to hold on to it through the whole extent of the great deep, now in the days of our strength, as ou ' 'athers held on to it in the days of our weakness. * * * I desire no war w h England. Far from us and them—from the world, indeed—far be such a calamity. But, sir, the way to avoid war is to stand up firmly and temperately for our clear rights. Submission never yet brought safety, and never will. To yield when clearly right is to abandon at once our interests and our honor, and to show the world how the finger of scorn can be best pointed at us.—*Hon. Lewis Cass* (Michigan), August 3.

There is that with nations whose fortune it is to have thriven and prospered under the assumption and exercise of rights which are not theirs, that they grow infatuated with their too-easily earned successes and become rash and daring and reckless in the extravagant conceit that whatever they wish to attain it is in their power to grasp, and that whatever they grasp is legitimately theirs. Such is England. She knows where lies the secret in the fountain of your power. She loathes to see those naval nurseries of yours, those hives of busy seamen pitched upon the waters of what she would have you call her seas, her gulfs, her bays, as so many advanced posts, watching over the deep. She can not but look with extreme jealousy and concern on the growing prosperity of this country, and think it were well for her if she could bar its progress while it has not yet reached its acme. * * *

Sir, what does England mean? Wha.. is she after? But, hush! She is negotiating. * * * She is negotiating. ' * * To negotiate under such circumstances were to sink in the dust what of pride, what of dignity, what of honor, we have grown to since we became a nation. * * * Until England has withdrawn her squadron, and gives satisfaction for what wrongs she may have perpetrated, let no negotiation be entertained, and if contrary to my expectation any has been entertained, let it be dropped at once and abandoned.—*Hon. Pierre Soulé* (Louisiana), August 12.

No patriots responded more readily to their country's call than the fishermen of New England. Who were the seamen in the two wars that guarded our coasts and captured the gallant ships of the British navy? They were mostly the fishermen of our country. Where were they educated for their duties? In the free schools of New England, or the banks of Newfoundland, and in the Gulf of St. Lawrence. Whence could these seamen have been supplied had not Congress, in its wisdom, encouraged the fishing industry?

In the small town of Marblehead alone "at the close of the Revolution there were more than thirteen hundred widows and fatherless children" who had been so rendered by deeds of war. At the close of the war of 1812 it is said that more than five hundred citizens of this town were released from on British prison. A celebrated fisherman of the State of Maine, Skipper Tucker, as he was called, captured more guns during the Revolutionary war than any naval commander in the service.

This, sir, is the class of men for whom I speak and whose industry I ask the Government to protect.—*Hon. Eno Scudder* (New Hampshire), August 12.

At this time the public of Canada were excited, and finally we came to the reciprocity treaty of 1854, a reciprocity treaty which I heard the honorable Senator from Alabama say that he regretted, as I understood him, was not in force now, a treaty that gave to the Canadian Government 94 per cent. of the advantage of the whole transaction as against 42 per cent. for us—94 per cent. on import duties was their advantage as against 42 per cent. for us. Subsequently that treaty was abandoned, and then came the treaty of 1871.

The treaty of 1871 is so familiar to everybody in the country that I shall not detain the Senate with any extended remarks upon it. Suffice it to say that we found that we had done just what the Senator from Texas [Mr. REAGAN] said as a member of the House a short time ago before he came into this body we always did. He said we had never made a treaty with Great Britain that we did not get the worst of it, although I have no doubt he will vote for this treaty. We found we had the worst of the treaty of 1871, and we found that we were ultimately compelled to pay at the rate of $500,000 a year for a privilege which, if the proof showed anything, it showed was of very little, if any, value at all. Then we abrogated that treaty. We abrogated it as soon as we could. We abrogated it by the course provided for in the treaty. In 1883 Congress passed a resolution in favor of its abrogation that took effect on the 1st of July, 1885.

When this Administration came into power it came in with this

question clear, as far as they were concerned without vexation. Congress
had said that the treaty of 1871 should be abrogated, and notice had
been given, and the 1st of July following the treaty was to be at an
end, or at least such portions of it as related to the fisheries.

There had been no demand made by anybody after the treaty of 1871
had been abrogated, by the men interested in fisheries, by the mer-
chants upon that coast or anywhere; nobody had suggested that we
had made a mistake, and nobody seemed to be anxious for the continuation of the old relations except the Canadians themselves. Seven
years before that time, in 1878, we had attempted to retire from it and
they had declined to allow us to do so; but nobody in 1885 wanted a
continuation of the treaty of 1871 save and except the Canadian Government and the British Government because the Canadians did,

So when this Administration came into power they came in un-
trammelled. There was no treaty; there was nothing to disturb them.
All they had to do was to do what their predecessors had done, insist
upon the same construction of the treaty of 1818 that we had always
contended for.

I do not forget that while the distinguished Senator from New York
[Mr. EVARTS] was serving the people in the capacity of Secretary of
State a difficulty arose with reference to this question, and I have not
forgotten and I think the country has not forgotten with what masterly
skill he handled the question, and how he brought the Canadians and
the British power to acknowledge the correctness of his position in accordance and in line with that of his illustrious predecessors, and how
he secured from the British Government a large payment of money to
indemnify the fishermen for losses they had sustained under an im-
proper construction of the treaty.

I know that the Senator from Alabama said that there had been no
redress furnished, that these outrages had been going on. Why, Mr.
President, the outrages were stopped when it was found that there was a
determination that they should stop, and the British not only quit, but
they paid for the damages they had caused.

Now, sir, what is our complaint against the Canadian and the British
Governments? I would not venture myself to formulate it, but in the
correspondence between our minister, Mr. Phelps, and the British authorities I find an admirable statement of our complaint, which I desire to read to the Senate. In writing to the Marquis of Salisbury on
the 26th day of July, 1887, Mr. Phelps, among other things, said:

> But what the United States Government complain of in these cases is that ex-
> isting regulations have been construed with a technical strictness, and enforced
> with a severity, in cases of inadvertent and accidental violation where no harm
> was done, which is both unusual and unnecessary, whereby the voyages of ves-
> sels have been broken up and heavy penalties incurred. That the liberal and
> reasonable construction of these laws that had prevailed for many years, and to
> which the fishermen had become accustomed, was changed without any notice
> given. And that every opportunity of unnecessary interference with the Amer-
> ican fishing vessels, to the prejudice and destruction of their business, has been
> availed of.

That is the gist of the complaints as made by our minister to England. I will present some other portions of this letter which bear on
the same subject, and also an extract from his letter of June 2, 1886, as
not only showing what we complain of, but the purpose for which these
outrages are committed.

[Complaint of Mr. Phelps to the Marquis of Salisbury, July 26, 1887.]

> Whether, in any of these cases, a technical violation of some requirement of
> law had, upon close and severe construction, taken place, it is not easy to deter-
> mine. But if such rules were generally enforced in such a manner in the ports

of the world, no vessel could sail in safety without carrying a solicitor versed in the intricacies of revenue and port regulations.

It is unnecessary to specify the various cases referred to, as the facts in many of them have been already laid before Her Majesty's Government.

Since the receipt of Lord Iddesleigh's note the United States Government has learned with grave regret that Her Majesty's assent has been given to the act of the Parliament of Canada, passed at its late session, entitled "An act further to amend the act respecting fishing by foreign vessels," which has been the subject of observation in the previous correspondence on the subject between the Governments of the United States and of Great Britain.

By the provisions of this act any foreign ship, vessel, or boat (whether engaged in fishing or not) found within any harbor in Canada, or within 3 marine miles of "any of the coasts, bays, or creeks of Canada," may be brought into port by any of the officers or persons mentioned in the act, her cargo searched, and her master examined upon oath touching the cargo and voyage under a heavy penalty if the questions asked are not truly answered; and if such ship has entered such waters "for any purpose not permitted by treaty or convention, or by law of the United Kingdom or of Canada, for the time being in force, such ship, vessel, or boat, and the tackle, rigging, apparel, furniture, stores, and cargo thereof shall be forfeited."

It has been pointed out in my note to Lord Iddesleigh, above mentioned, that the 3-mile limit referred to in this act is claimed by the Canadian Government to include considerable portions of the high seas, such as the Bay of Fundy, the Bay of Chaleur, and similar waters, by drawing the line from headland to headland, and that American fishermen had been excluded from those waters accordingly.

It has been seen also that the term "any purpose not permitted by treaty" is held by that Government to comprehend every possible act of human intercourse, except only the four purposes named in the treaty—shelter, repairs, wood, and water.

Under the provisions of the recent act, therefore, and the Canadian interpretation of the treaty, any American fishing vessel that may venture into a Canadian harbor, or may have occasion to pass through the very extensive waters thus comprehended, may be seized at the discretion of any one of numerous subordinate officers, carried into port, subjected to search and the examination of her master upon oath, her voyage broken up, and the vessel and cargo confiscated, if it shall be determined by the local authorities that she has ever even posted or received a letter or landed a passenger in any part of Her Majesty's dominions in America.

And it is publicly announced in Canada that a larger fleet of cruisers is being prepared by the authorities and that greater vigilance will be exerted on their part in the next fishing season than in the last.

It is in the act to which the one above referred to is an amendment that is found the provision to which I drew attention in a note to Lord Iddesleigh of December 2, 1886, by which it is enacted that in case a dispute arises as to whether any seizure has or has not been legally made, the burden of proving the illegality of the seizure shall be upon the owner or claimant.

In his reply to that note of January 11, 1887, his lordship intimates that this provision is intended only to impose upon a person claiming a license the burden of proving it. But a reference to the act shows that such is by no means the restriction of the enactment. It refers in the broadest and clearest terms to any seizure that is made under the provisions of the act, which covers the whole subject of protection against illegal fishing; and it applies not only to the proof of a license to fish, but to all questions of fact whatever, necessary to a determination as to the legality of a seizure or the authority of the person making it.

[Complaint of Mr. Phelps to Lord Rosebery, June 2, 1886.]

Recurring, then, to the only real question in the case, whether the vessel is to be forfeited for purchasing bait of an inhabitant of Nova Scotia, to be used in lawful fishing, it may be readily admitted that if the language of the treaty of 1818 is to be interpreted literally, rather than according to its spirit and plain intent, a vessel engaged in fishing would be prohibited from entering a Canadian port "for any purpose whatever" except to obtain wood or water, to repair damages, or to seek shelter. Whether it would be liable to the extreme penalty of confiscation for a breach of this prohibition in a trifling and harmless instance might be quite another question.

Such a literal construction is best refuted by considering its preposterous consequences. If a vessel enters a port to post a letter, or send a telegram, or buy a newspaper, to obtain a physician in case of illness, or a surgeon in case of accident, to land or bring off a passenger, or even to lend assistance to the inhabitants in fire, flood, or pestilence, it would, upon this construction, be held to violate the treaty stipulations maintained between two enlightened maritime and most friendly nations, whose ports are freely open to each other in all other places and under all other circumstances. If a vessel is not engaged in fishing she may enter all ports; but if employed in fishing, not denied to be lawful, she

Is excluded, though on the most innocent errand. She may buy water, but not food or medicine; wood, but not coal. She may repair rigging, but not purchase a new rope, though the inhabitants are desirous to sell it. If she even entered the port (having no other business) to report herself to the custom-house as the vessel in question is now seized for not doing, she would be equally within the interdiction of the treaty. If it be said these are extreme instances of violation of the treaty not likely to be insisted on, I reply that no one of them is more extreme than the one relied upon in this case.

Mr. President, the question comes, What are the Canadians after? Why have they boarded within two years more than two thousand American fishing vessels? Why have they gone upon American vessels in number more than two thousand, charging them with violation of either international law, or the treaty, or local law? For what purpose? It has been asserted here, and it is not denied, that it was for the purpose of compelling us to accept a reciprocity treaty from them, as they did get one from us in 1854 and 1871. The Senator from Maine [Mr. FRYE] asserted that; the Senator from Alabama [Mr. MORGAN] admitted it; but we have authority equally good. The Democratic Administration has asserted it and declared that that was the purpose. Mr. Bayard, in a letter to Mr. Phelps, of February 8, 1887, amongst other things, said:

At page 15 of the printed inclosure and in the last paragraph will be found the explicit avowal of claim by the Canadian Government to employ the convention of 1818 as an instrument of interference with the exercise of open-sea fishing by citizens of the United States, and to give it such a construction as will enable the fishermen of the provinces better to compete at less "disadvantage in the markets of the United States" in the pursuit of the deep-sea fisheries.

At the outset of this discussion, in my note to Sir Lionel West, of May 10, 1886, I said:

"The question, therefore, arises whether such a construction is admissible as would convert the treaty of 1818 from being an instrumentality for the protection of the inshore fisheries along the described parts of the British American coasts into a pretext or means of obstructing the business of deep-sea fishing by citizens of the United States, and of interrupting and destroying the commercial intercourse that since the treaty of 1818, and independent of any treaty whatever, has grown up and now exists under the concurrent and friendly laws and mercantile regulations of the respective countries."

When I wrote this I hardly expected that the motives I suggested, rather than imputed, would be admitted by the authorities of the provinces, and was entirely unprepared for a distinct avowal thereof, not only as regards the obstruction of deep-sea fishing operations by our fishermen, but also in respect of their independent commercial intercourse, yet it will be seen that the Canadian minister of justice avers that it is "most prejudicial" to the interests of the provinces "that United States fishermen should be permitted to come into their harbors on any pretext."

The correspondence now sent to you, together with others relating to the same subject that has taken place since the President's message of December 8, communicating the same to Congress, will be laid before Congress without delay, and will assist the two Houses materially in the legislation proposed for the security of the rights of American fishing vessels under treaty and international law and comity.

I am, etc.,

                                                    T. F. BAYARD

Mr. Phelps, the American minister, in a letter to Lord Rosebery of June 2, 1886, which will be found in Senate Executive Document No. 113, page 415, amongst other things, said:

The real source of the difficulty that has arisen is well understood. It is to be found in the irritation that has taken place among a portion of the Canadian people on account of the termination by the United States Government of the treaty of Washington on the 1st of July last, whereby fish imported from Canada into the United States, and which so long as that treaty remained in force was admitted free, is now liable to the import duty provided by the general revenue laws, and the opinion appears to have gained ground in Canada that the United States may be driven, by harassing and annoying their fishermen, into the adoption of a new treaty by which Canadian fish shall be admitted free.

He adds:

It is not necessary to say that this scheme is likely to prove as mistaken in policy as it is indefensible in principle. In terminating the treaty of Washington the United States were simply exercising a right expressly reserved to both parties by the treaty itself, and of the exercise of which by either party neither can complain. They will not be coerced by wanton injury into the making of a new one, nor would a negotiation that had its origin in mutual irritation be promising of success. The question now is, not what fresh treaty may or might be desirable, but what is the true and just construction as between the two nations of the treaty that already exists.

That was the sentiment of the American Senate as expressed in the Frye resolution, and which found advocacy on the other side of the Chamber, notably by the Senator from Alabama, who declared over and over again in his speech, as I propose to quote before I quit, that we needed no new treaty; that all we needed and all we wanted was a proper construction of the treaty of 1818, which he declared was not difficult to make; and he went further and said, as I will show, that if it was left to him to add to it, he knew nothing that he could add that would make it more certain.

Again, on page 36 of the same document, Mr. Phelps to the Marquis of Salisbury, in his letter of January 26, 1887, said:

The United States Government is not able to concur in the favorable view taken by Lord Iddesleigh of the efforts of the Canadian Government "to promote a friendly negotiation." That the conduct of that Government has been directed to obtaining a revision of the existing treaty is not to be doubted; but its efforts have been of such a character as to preclude the prospect of a successful negotiation so long as they continue, and seriously to endanger the friendly relations between the United States and Great Britain.

Aside from the question as to the right of American vessels to purchase bait in Canadian ports, such a construction has been given to the treaty between the United States and Great Britain as amounts virtually to a declaration of almost complete non-intercourse with American vessels. The usual comity between friendly nations has been refused in their case, and in one instance, at least, the ordinary offices of humanity. The treaty of friendship and amity which, in return for very important concessions by the United States to Great Britain, reserved to the American vessels certain specified privileges has been construed to exclude them from all other intercourse common to civilized life and to universal maritime usage among nations not at war, as well as from the right to touch and trade accorded to all other vessels.

And quite aside from any question arising upon construction of the treaty, the provisions of the custom-house acts and regulations have been systematically enforced against American ships for alleged petty and technical violations of legal requirements in a manner so unreasonable, unfriendly, and unjust as to render the privileges accorded by the treaty practically nugatory.

* * * * *

It has been seen also that the term "any purpose not permitted by treaty" is held by that Government to comprehend every possible act of human intercourse, except only the four purposes named in the treaty—shelter, repairs, wood, and water.

Under the provisions of the recent act, therefore, and the Canadian interpretation of the treaty, any American fishing vessel that may venture into a Canadian harbor, or may have occasion to pass through the very extensive waters thus comprehended, may be seized at the discretion of any one of numerous subordinate officers, carried into port, subjected to search and the examination of her master upon oath, her voyage broken up, and the vessel and cargo confiscated. If it shall be determined by the local authorities that she has ever even posted or received a letter or landed a passenger in any part of Her Majesty's dominions in America.

In a letter of Mr. Phelps to Earl Iddesleigh, September 11, 1886, page 433, our minister said:

The conduct of the provincial officers toward these vessels was therefore not merely unfriendly and injurious, but in clear and plain violation of the terms of the treaty. And I am instructed to say that reparation for the losses sustained by it to the owners of the vessels will be claimed by the United States Government on their behalf as soon as the amount can be accurately ascertained.

It will be observed that interference with American fishing vessels by Canadian authorities is becoming more and more frequent, and more and more flagrant in its disregard of treaty obligations and of the principles of comity and friendly intercourse. The forbearance and moderation of the United States Government in respect to them appear to have been misunderstood and to have been taken advantage of by the provincial government. The course of the

United States has been dictated, not only by an anxious desire to preserve friendly relations, but by the full confidence that the interposition of Her Majesty's Government would be such as to put a stop to the transactions complained of, and to afford reparation for what has already taken place. The subject has become one of grave importance, and I earnestly solicit the immediate attention of your lordship to the question it involves, and to the views presented in my former note and in those of the Secretary of State.

Again on June 2, 1886, in a letter to Lord Rosebery, Mr. Phelps used this language, on page 419 of the document to which I have already referred:

From all the circumstances attending this case, and other recent cases like it, it seems to me very apparent that the seizure was not made for the purpose of enforcing any right or redressing any wrong. As I have before remarked, it is not pretended that the vessel had been engaged in fishing, or was intending to fish in the prohibited waters, or that it had done or was intending to do any other injurious act. It was proceeding upon its regular and lawful business of fishing in the deep sea. It had received no request, and of course could have disregarded no request, to depart, and was, in fact, departing when seized; nor had its master refused to answer any questions put by the authorities. It had violated no existing law, and had incurred no penalty that any known statute imposed.

It seems to me impossible to escape the conclusion that this and other similar seizures were made by the Canadian authorities for the deliberate purpose of harassing and embarrassing the American fishing vessels in the pursuit of their lawful employment. And the injury, which would have been a serious one, if committed under a mistake, is very much aggravated by the motives which appear to have prompted it.

I am instructed by my Government earnestly to protest against these proceedings as wholly unwarranted by the treaty of 1818, and altogether inconsistent with the friendly relations hitherto existing between the United States and Her Majesty's Government; to request that the David J. Adams, and the other American fishing vessels now under seizure in Canadian ports, be immediately released, and that proper orders may be issued to prevent similar proceedings in the future. And I am also instructed to inform you that the United States will hold Her Majesty's Government responsible for all losses which may be sustained by American citizens in the dispossession of their property growing out of the search, seizure, detention, or sale of their vessels lawfully within the territorial waters of British North America.

The real source of the difficulty that has arisen is well understood. It is to be found in the irritation that has taken place among a portion of the Canadian people on account of the termination by the United States Government of the treaty of Washington on the 1st of July last, whereby fish imported from Canada into the United States, and which so long as that treaty was in force was admitted free, is now liable to the import duty provided by the general revenue laws, and the opinion appears to have gained ground in Canada that the United States may be driven, by harassing and annoying their fishermen, into the adoption of a new treaty by which Canadian fish shall be admitted free.

It is not necessary to say that this scheme is likely to prove as mistaken in policy as it is indefensible in principle. In terminating the treaty of Washington the United States were simply exercising a right expressly reserved to both parties by the treaty itself, and of the exercise of which by either party neither can complain. They will not be coerced by wanton injury into the making of a new one. Nor would a negotiation that had its origin in mutual irritation be promising of success. The question now is, not what fresh treaty may or might be desirable, but what is the true and just construction, as between the two nations, of the treaty that already exists?

The Government of the United States, approaching this question in the most friendly spirit, can not doubt that it will be met by Her Majesty's Government in the same spirit, and feels every confidence that the action of Her Majesty's Government in the premises will be such as to maintain the cordial relations between the two countries that have so long happily prevailed.

I have the honor to be, etc.,

E. J. PHELPS.

Mr. President, it can not be denied in regard to these outrages perpetrated upon the American fishermen, by which they have been seized and taken into British ports and outraged generally—conduct of which the late Secretary of the Treasury, Mr. Manning, in a letter that he addressed the House of Representatives in 1886, declared over his official signature was brutal; that has been characterized by the Secretary o' . . . . . by our minister to London to the very extreme of diplomatic language as being in violation of treaty, contrary to good morals, and an indignity to this great and independent people—it can not be denied (because you have the authority of the Administration as well as the consensus of all that have been interested and have studied and discussed the question) that this movement is not for the purpose of enforcing the treaty stipulations of 1818, but to compel us to make a treaty, whether we will or not, that they think is in the interest of Canada and the British dominion on our north.

Can we afford under such circumstances to negotiate? Could we afford to call a commission to our national capital to consider subjects of dispute when the Secretary of State himself is on record and his minister is on record that these are outrages perpetrated for the purpose of creating a necessity in the minds of the American people for a new treaty? Was not Mr. Phelps right when he said we do not want any new treaty under existing circumstances? Was he not correct when he said it is not now a question what kind of treaty is desirable provided we were in a condition to treat, but what is the proper construction of the treaty of 1818?

But, Mr. President, I say, and believe the American people will say with one voice when they understand this question, that it was beneath the dignity of the United States to enter into negotiation until at least the other side should have ceased to commit these grievances against us. We should not complain of an honest construction, although wrong, but when the Secretary of State tells them and his minister tells them that they know that this is but a pretense on their part; that there is not any such construction in their view of the law; that these are not proceedings instigated by a desire to protect their rights, but to inflict injuries upon us to compel us to pursue a course that they think will inure to their benefit, I say that we can not and ought not to have treated, and so said the Administration. Mr. Phelps, in a letter to Lord Iddesleigh on September 11, 1886, says, on page 433:

The proposal in your lordship's note that a revision of the treaty stipulations bearing upon the subject of the fisheries should be attempted by the Government upon the basis of mutual concessions is one that under other circumstances would merit and receive serious consideration. Such a revision was desired by the Government of the United States before the present disputes arose, and when there was a reasonable prospect that it might have been carried into effect. Various reasons not within its control now concur to make the present time inopportune for that purpose, and greatly to diminish the hope of a favorable result to such an effort. Not the least of them is the irritation produced in the United States by the course of the Canadian Government, and the belief thereby engendered that a new treaty is attempted to be forced upon the United States Government.

It seems apparent that the questions now presented and the transactions that are the subject of present complaint must be considered and adjusted upon the provisions of the existing treaty, and upon the construction that is to be given to them.

A just construction of these stipulations, and such as would consist with the dignity, the interests, and the friendly relations of the two countries, ought not to be difficult, and can doubtless be arrived at.

Later, on January 26, 1887, page 437, speaking of this same subject, whether the Government of the United States could now treat, he said:

The reasons why a revision of the treaty of 1818 can not now, in the opinion of the United States Government, be hopefully undertaken, and which are set forth in my note to Lord Iddesleigh of September 11, have increased in force since that note was written.

Thus, Mr. President, we have the authority of the Administration itself, that until redress for these outrages had been in some way obtained by us, or they had been overlooked or forgiven at the request of the people who committed them, we ought not to have any treaty at all.

I must retrace my steps a little, and come back to the condition of affairs when the Administration came into power.

As I said before, this Administration was met by an expiring treaty on July 1, 1885. Eight days after this Administration came into power the British minister addressed a most remarkable note to the Secretary of State.

Congress had declared that the treaty of 1871 should come to an end; there had been practical unanimity everywhere on the subject; and yet the British minister on the 12th day of March, 1885, eight days after the Administration came into power, makes a suggestion to the Administration substantially that Congress did not know what it wanted, that the great Government of the United States represented in its legislative department was not capable of determining these questions as they ought to be, and that the State Department and he might be able to work out something that would be better. Can anybody believe, does anybody believe that this letter which I shall read could ever have been submitted by Mr. West of his own volition? Would there have been that temerity on the part of any representative from abroad to have said to an executive officer of the United States, "Your Government has made a mistake in a matter of internal policy," with which he had no concern? I think it may be fairly presumed that he got his idea from the Administration, that they were prepared to negotiate upon this subject with a view to a change of status. He said—I read from page 484 of the same document:

1.—*Mr. West's memorandum of March 12, 1885.*

[Memorandum.—Confidential.]

The fishery clauses of the treaty of Washington of 1871 will expire on the 1st of July next. It has been represented by the Canadian Government that much inconvenience is likely to arise in consequence, unless some agreement can be made for an extension of the period.

When the time comes (1st of July next) American ships will be actually engaged in fishing within the territorial waters of the Dominion. These vessels will have been fitted out for the season's fishing and have made all their usual arrangements for following it up until its termination in the autumn. If, under these circumstances, the provincial or municipal authorities in Canada were to insist upon their strict rights, and to compel such vessels, under pain of seizure, to desist from fishing, considerable hardship would be occasioned to the owners, and a feeling of bitterness engendered on both sides, which it is clearly the interest of both Governments to avert.

It seems, therefore, desirable, in order to avoid such possible complications, that both Governments should come to an agreement under which the clauses might be in effect extended until the 1st of January, 1886.

If this were done the existing state of things would come to an end at a date between the fishery season of 1885 and that of 1886, and an abrupt transition at a moment when fishery operations were being carried on would be thus avoided.

WASHINGTON, *March 12, 1885.*

The solicitude of the Canadian Government for our fishermen was hardly in keeping with their subsequent conduct, hardly in keeping with their conduct years ago, and it can not be misunderstood that this negotiation was commenced and carried on for an entirely different purpose, as I shall show in a moment as briefly as I can, for the purpose of getting from us that which the Canadian Government had been demanding, a reciprocity treaty, and that the Administration were parties to this, and that the Secretary of State understood it. His letters show that it was not a simple question of fishing, but it was more than that.

On the 22d day of April, 1885, Mr. Bayard replied. Whether there had been any other correspondence I know not, except that it is not found in the diplomatic correspondence sent to the Senate.

2.—Mr. Bayard to Mr. West, April 22, 1885.

[Memorandum of April 22, 1885.—Personal.]

DEPARTMENT OF STATE, Washington, April 22, 1885.

DEAR MR. WEST: I have on several occasions lately, in conversation, acquainted you with my interest in the fisheries memorandum which accompanied your personal letter of March 12.

Several informal talks I have had with Sir Ambrose Shea have enabled me to formulate the views of this Government upon the proposition made in behalf of the Dominion and the Province of Newfoundland, and I take pleasure in handing you herewith a memorandum embodying the results. If this suits, I shall be happy to confirm the arrangement by an exchange of notes at your earliest convenience.

I am, my dear Mr. West, very sincerely yours,

T. F. BAYARD.

The Hon. L. S. SACKVILLE WEST, etc.

I do not know very much about the intricacies of diplomacy and I do not know very much about the negotiation of treaties, but it struck me as a very singular proposition that the Secretary of State, upon a subject which had engrossed the attention of all his predecessors for several years on and off, that had engrossed the attention of Congress, should have needed the views of Sir Ambrose Shea, who, I understand, is a member of the cabinet of one of the British provinces. At all events the memorandum is the result of informal talks of the Secretary with Sir Ambrose Shea. How much of it is the work of Sir Ambrose Shea and how much of it is the work of the Administration I do not know. So I am unable to give the proper credit.

I find on June 13, 1885, another memorandum:

3.—Mr. West's memoranda of June 13, 1885.

[Memoranda.]

It is proposed to state in notes according temporary arrangements respecting fisheries that an agreement has been arrived at under circumstances affording prospect of negotiation for development and extension of trade between the United States and British North America—

That is the whole question in a nut-shell—

affording prospect of negotiation for development and extension of trade between the United States and British North America.

I submit that means reciprocity and does not mean anything else. This was the initiatory step towards a reciprocity treaty with Great Britain. Mr. West added:

The government of Newfoundland do not make refunding of duties a condition of their acceptance of the proposed agreement, but they rely on it having due consideration before the International commission which may be appointed.

To that Mr. Bayard replied, June 19, 1885:

[Confidential.]

DEPARTMENT OF STATE, Washington, June 19, 1885.

MY DEAR MR. WEST: I assume that the two confidential memoranda you handed to me on the 13th instant embrace the acceptance by the Dominion and the British-American coast provinces of the general features of my memorandum of April 21, concerning a temporary arrangement respecting the fisheries, with the understanding expressed on their side that the "agreement has been arrived at under circumstances affording prospect of negotiation for development and extension of trade between the United States and British North America."

To such a contingent understanding I can have no objection. Indeed, I regard it as covered by the statement in my memorandum of May 21, that the ar-

rangement therein contemplated would be reached " with the understanding
that the President of the United States would bring the whole question of the
fisheries before Congress at its next session in December, and recommend the
appointment of a commission in which the Governments of the United States
and of Great Britain should be respectively represented, which commission
should be charged with the consideration and settlement upon a just, equitable,
and honorable basis, of the entire question of the fishing rights of the two Governments and their respective citizens on the coasts of the United States and
British North America."

The equities of the question being before such a mixed commission would
doubtless have the fullest latitude of expression and treatment on both sides;
and the purpose in view being the maintenance of good neighborhood and intercourse between the two countries, the recommendation of any measures
which the commission might deem necessary to attain those ends would seem
to fall within its province, and such recommendations could not fail to receive
attentive consideration. I am not, therefore, prepared to state limits to the
proposals to be brought forward in the suggested commission on behalf of either
party.

I believe this statement will be satisfactory to you, and I should be pleased
to be informed at the earliest day practicable of your acceptance of the understanding on behalf of British North America; and by this simple exchange of
notes and memoranda the agreement will be completed in season to enable the
President to make the result publicly known to the citizens engaged in the fishing on the British-American Atlantic coast.

I have the honor to be, with the highest respect, sir, your obedient servant,
T. F. BAYARD.

Hon. L. S. SACKVILLE WEST.

That was not entirely satisfactory to Mr. West, and he replied on
the 20th:

Mr. West to Mr. Bayard, June 20, 1885.

[Confidential.]

BRITISH LEGATION, *Washington, June 20, 1885.*

MY DEAR MR. BAYARD: I beg to acknowledge the receipt of your confidential note of yesterday's date, concerning the proposed temporary arrangement
respecting the fisheries, which I am authorized by Her Majesty's Government
to negotiate with you on behalf of the Government of the Dominion of Canada
and the government of Newfoundland, to be effected by an exchange of notes
founded on your memorandum of the 21st of April last.

The two confidential memoranda which I handed to you on the 13th instant
contain, as you assume, the acceptance by the Dominion and the British-American coast provinces of the general features of your above-mentioned memorandum, with the understanding expressed on their side that the agreement has
been arrived at under circumstances affording prospects of negotiation for the
development and extension of trade between the United States and British North
America, a contingent understanding to which, as you state, you can have no
objection, as you regard it as covered by the terms of your memorandum of
April 21.

In authorizing me to negotiate this agreement, Earl Granville states, as I have
already had occasion to intimate to you, that it is on the distinct understanding that it is a temporary one, and that its conclusion must not be held to preju-
dice any claim which may be advanced to more satisfactory equivalents by the
colonial governments in the course of the negotiation for a more permanent
settlement. Earl Granville further wishes me to tell you that Her Majesty's
Government and the colonial governments have consented to the arrangement
solely as a mark of good-will to the Government and people of the United
States—

A remarkable exhibition of good-will to the people of the United
States to give them that which they had declared without dissent,
through the only organ through which they could properly declare it,
that they did not want it continued—

and to avoid difficulties which might be raised by the termination of the fishery
articles in the midst of a fishing season; and also the acceptance of such a *modus
vivendi* does not, by any implication, affect the value of the inshore fisheries by
the Governments of Canada and Newfoundland. I had occasion to remark to
you that while the colonial governments are asked to guaranty immunity from
interference to American vessels resorting to Canadian waters, no such immunity is offered in your memorandum to Canadian vessels resorting to American
waters, but that the Dominion government presumed that the agreement in this
respect would be mutual. As you accepted this view, it would, I think, be as
well that mention should be made to this effect in the notes.

21

Under the reservations, as above indicated, in which I believe you acquiesce, I am prepared to accept the understanding on behalf of British North America, and to exchange notes in the above sense.

I have the honor to be, with the highest respect, sir, your obedient servant,
L. S. SACKVILLE WEST.

Hon. T. E. BAYARD, etc.

So, Mr. President, I think it may be assumed that the initiative of this proposed treaty was not for the purpose of making a treaty on the fishery question, but a reciprocity treaty. The President of the United States, agreeable to his agreement with the British Government, submitted a proposition to Congress for the appointment of a commission. I need not go into that at any great length, except to show the action of certain members of the Senate of the United States upon that proposition. The Senator from Maine [Mr. FRYE] offered this resolution:

Resolved, That, in the opinion of the Senate, the appointment of a commission in which the Governments of the United States and Great Britain shall be represented, charged with the consideration and settlement of the fishing rights of the two Governments, on the coasts of the United States and British North America, ought not to be provided for by Congress.

When that resolution was before the Senate the Committee on Foreign Relations were represented not in a partisan way at all. The Senator from Maine made some remarks, which were followed by the Senator from Alabama, a member, and I may say the leading member of the committee upon the Democratic side. Mr. MORGAN said:

In listening to the remarks of the Senator from Maine, and also in what investigation I have been able to give this subject, I am unable to ascertain that there is really any unsettled question between the United States and Great Britain in regard to the fisheries of the northeastern coast. I have inquired of Senators who have had long experience in diplomatic affairs of the country, to ascertain, if I could, whether there was any open question of damages, any claim of damages arising between the Governments respectively out of any supposed breach of our fisheries treaties or our fisheries laws; and I can hear nothing of that kind. The Halifax Commission seems to have settled for good and all every controversy, sounding in damages at least, which has been promoted or urged by the citizens of the countries on either side.

I conceive that there is no want of certainty in our treaty relations, and there is scarcely room for a difference in interpretation of what our treaty relations actually are. The two treaties which have settled the actual and what we might term the permanent rights of the people of the United States and of the Dominion country in regard to the fisheries are the treaties of 1783 and 1818. No other treaties we have made at all in respect to the fisheries have undertaken to define the permanent enduring rights either of the British people or of our people in respect of the fisheries. We have had two other treaties on this subject, the treaty of 1854 and the treaty of 1871, but they were both temporary in their character and both made liable to be suspended by the action of either government after they had run for ten years, and both have been abrogated. So that the field is entirely clear in respect of the actual state of treaty relations between the United States and Great Britain, and those treaty relations rest upon the treaties of 1783 and 1818.

He then discussed the question whether the treaty of 1783 had been superseded by the treaty of 1818, and he differed from the Senator from Delaware [Mr. GRAY] and some others, and asserted that it had not been. He quoted the treaty of 1783, and declared:

That was all that was said about it. A broader right of fishery than that cannot be conceived of; no restriction or restraint upon it at all, except that in conducting their business they should not trespass or intrude on private property on the shore in drawing their fish or mending their nets or whatever other use they might have for the shore.

He went on to say in substance that it was an entire perversion of the treaty of 1818 to give it the construction that the British or Canadian authorities were contending for. Then he said, speaking of the British statute:

If that is so, it seems to me there is no difficulty at all either in construing or in handling this matter. As I remarked before, I can not see that there is any difficulty in the construction of the treaty of mistaken by itself. All the rights that are guarantied there and that have not been enlarged by statute of Great Britain obtain, and there is no difficulty in the construction of them. There is no difficulty in the construction of the British statutes on this subject. But, then, we are not called upon to construe them. What we are called upon to do is to protect our people against any wrong construction that they may put upon their own laws, by a power that we reserve expressly in the hands of the President of the United States.

I do not wish to volunteer any opinions about this subject before a question gets before the Senate and I am compelled to act upon it; but my convictions are very strong; they are fixed; indeed I may say that we can get along with the people of Great Britain on this subject without any further treaty at all and without any further legislation. If any one were to ask me what provision of a treaty I would frame to compose and settle any question of fundamental law between us and Great Britain in respect of the fisheries, I could not suggest it, or if I were asked to propose an amendment to the statutes of the United States so as to put the control of this intricate subject more completely in the hands of our own Government I could not frame the amendment to the statutes. I would not know how to do it. I believe that both the treaty stipulations and the situation under the statutes are about as complete as we are ever able to make them. There may be other interests, and there are other interests lying between the people of the British possessions and the United States that I would like very much indeed to see promoted by further negotiation, but I can not call to mind, there is no suggestion to my mind of, any improvement that we could make under existing conditions of our rights in the fisheries of that Northeastern coast.

Speaking on another point he said:

Therefore I think that the Government should leave the matter just where it is, and I do not think Congress can be persuaded to repeal that act.

That was an act which gave the President power to interfere if our ships were not properly treated.

That was the opinion of the Senator from Alabama when he declared that our commercial rights were derived from the act of Great Britain of 1830 in conjunction with our own, when he declared in unequivocal terms that the right to purchase bait and ice were guarantied to us by that commercial arrangement, and as long as Great Britain did not retire from that arrangement made between the British Government and ours by which we were to pass certain legislation and they were to have certain orders made in council, there was no question at all about our right to buy ice and bait. He went on to say that it was beneath the dignity of the Government of the United States to put in a treaty a provision that we might buy bait and ice.

This resolution, as everybody remembers, passed with practical unanimity or nearly so, there being but ten votes against it in the Senate and the Senator from Alabama being one of those who voted for it.

However, Mr. President, these violations of our treaty rights continued and it was thought best to arm the Government of the United States with more extended powers than the acts already on the statute-book gave. A bill was introduced, if I recollect aright, by the Senator from Vermont [Mr. EDMUNDS] and referred to the Committee on Foreign Relations, of which the Senator from Alabama, as I have before said, is a member, and when the bill came before the Senate the Senator from Alabama said:

Mr. President, I was a member of the committee who reported this bill, and it received my cordial approbation. I was also a member of the subcommittee which formulated the bill, and it was carefully considered there in connection with the evidence which had been collected not only from their own investigations under the order of the Senate but also from the archives of the State Department as far as we had access to those archives.

Mr. President, I call the attention of the Senate to this statement made by the Senator from Alabama that he was one of the originators of this act that armed the President with power to suspend Canadian commerce if he saw fit.

I call the attention of the Senate to that because I propose to notice
of complaint made in the Senate that we had acted cowardly in this
matter, that we were not willing to take the responsibility of deter
mining whether there were violations of the treaty of 1818, and were
not willing ourselves to declare non-intercourse, either limited or to an
extended degree, but that we had imposed this upon the President, as
he said, for the purpose of getting the President into difficulty, or words
to that effect. Yet he announced to the Senate that he was one of the
originators of it, and that it had his unqualified support; and he defended it in a lengthy speech, I need not say in an able speech. He
took the American side of the question, and when the Senator from
Maryland [Mr. GORMAN] attempted to amend the statute of March 3,
1887, by giving it more force, as he said, and extending it further, the
Senator from Alabama was again heard. On all occasions it received
his unqualified approbation as it received the unqualified approbation
of every member of the Democratic party in the Senate. No man on
that side either lifted his voice against the bill or voted against it; and
yet we are told now that the statute was enacted for the purpose of getting the Democratic Administration into difficulty.

When the bill went to the House of Representatives it was ably discussed, as the RECORD will show. Not wishing to detain the Senate,
I shall not advert to each particular statement made by the members
of the House. I presume Senators have looked up that debate. There
was no objection to the bill. There was a controversy between the
House and the Senate as to which particular bill should be adopted,
whether it should be the bill of the Senate or the bill of the House.
It was contended in the House that the House bill was the most
vigorous, that it put more power in the hands of the Administration,
and therefore they favored it. In the House at that time there was
the present Senator from Virginia [Mr. DANIEL], who made an able
speech in defense of the American idea of the treaty of 1818; there
was the junior Senator from Texas [Mr. REAGAN], who declared
that we ought to be careful how we dealt with Great Britain, for
in all our dealings with Great Britain we had been always over-
reached; there were Mr. CLEMENTS, Mr. COX, and other distinguished Democrats, all of them, including Mr. MILLS, supporting the
measure, not simply by their votes, but by their speeches, every one
of them insisting then that the American construction of the treaty of
1818 was the construction we should insist upon at all times. That
bill passed the Senate with one dissenting vote, and he was not a Democrat.

Mr. FRYE. That was a vote cast by mistake.

Mr. TELLER. The Senator from Maine says that was a vote cast
by mistake. The bill passed the House with one dissenting vote, and
I do not know whose vote that was.

I desire to submit several letters of the Secretary of State for the purpose of showing that when we complain and say that the conduct of
the Canadian officials has been in violation of the treaty we are supported by the Secretary of State. I find that in a letter to Mr. West,
written May 10, 1886, he declares that the British construction of the
treaty, if allowed, would be in effect to utterly destroy all our rights
under the treaty of 1818. He was insisting in the letter as to our commercial rights that they had been enlarged by the action of Congress,
the proclamation of the President and the action of the British Government in 1830, and that they included fishing vessels as well as other
vessels. He said, on page 290:

President Jackson's proclamation of October 5, 1830, created a reciprocal commercial intercourse, on terms of perfect equality of flag, between this country and the British American dependencies, by repealing the navigation acts of April 18, 1818, May 15, 1820, and March 1, 1823, and admitting British vessels and their cargoes "to an entry in the ports of the United States from the islands, provinces, and colonies of Great Britain on or near the American continent, and north or east of the United States." These commercial privileges have since received a large extension in the interests of propinquity, and in some cases favors have been granted by the United States without equivalent concession. Of the latter class is the exemption granted by the shipping act of June 26, 1884, amounting to one-half of the regular tonnage dues on all vessels from the British North American and West Indian possessions entering ports of the United States. Of the reciprocal class are the arrangements for transit of goods, and the remission, by proclamation, as to certain British ports and places of the remainder of the tonnage-tax, on evidence of equal treatment being shown to our vessels.

On the other side, British and colonial legislation, as notably in the case of the imperial shipping and navigation act of June 26, 1849, has contributed its share toward building up an intimate intercourse and beneficial traffic between the two countries founded on mutual interest and convenience.

Again he said, on page 291:

The effect of this colonial legislation and Executive interpretation, if executed according to the letter, would be not only to expand the restrictions and renunciations of the treaty of 1818, which related solely to inshore fishery within the 3-mile limit, so as to affect the deep-sea fisheries, the right to which remained unquestioned and unimpaired for the enjoyment of the citizens of the United States, but further to diminish and practically to destroy the privileges expressly secured to American fishing vessels to visit those inshore waters for the objects of shelter, repair of damages, and purchasing wood and obtaining water.

Again he said, on page 292:

I may recall to your attention the fact that a proposition to exclude the vessels of the United States engaged in fishing from carrying also merchandise was made by the British negotiators of the treaty of 1818, but, being resisted by the American negotiators, was abandoned. This fact would seem clearly to indicate that the business of fishing did not then and does not now disqualify a vessel from also trading in the regular ports of entry.

On the 29th of May, 1886, in a letter to Mr. West, Mr. Bayard used this language, on page 297:

SIR: I have just received an official imprint of House of Commons bill No. 136, now pending in the Canadian Parliament, entitled "An act further to amend the act respecting fishing by foreign vessels," and am informed that it has passed the house and is now pending in the senate.

This bill proposes the forcible search, seizure, and forfeiture of any foreign vessel within any harbor in Canada, or hovering within 3 marine miles of any of the coasts, bays, creeks, or harbors in Canada, where such vessel has entered such waters for any purpose not permitted by the laws of nations, or by treaty or convention, or by any law of the United Kingdom or of Canada now in force.

*   *   *   *   *   *   *

Such proceedings I conceive to be flagrantly violative of the reciprocal commercial privileges to which citizens of the United States are lawfully entitled under statutes of Great Britain and the well-defined and publicly proclaimed authority of both countries, besides being in respect of the existing conventions between the two countries an assumption of jurisdiction entirely unwarranted and which is wholly denied by the United States.

The contention of the Department of State is new that we never had any commercial rights for our fishing vessels. What did the Secretary of State mean when he was thus addressing the British authorities as the representative of the Government of the United States? Was he in earnest? Did he believe that we had commercial rights?

It will be seen that the Secretary of State notified the citizens of the United States that their right to buy bait in the Canadian ports was unquestioned under the law; and to-day we are told by the President, by the Secretary of State, and by all his adherents on the other side of the Chamber, that it is a right we never had at all. If we assert that the right exists by virtue of the treaty, we are told that our partisan zeal to secure votes in certain quarters is so great that we can not approach this subject in the judicial temper with which they are approaching it.

Again, the Secretary of State said on the 7th of June, 1886, page 298:

Sir: I regret exceedingly to communicate that report is to-day made to me, accompanied by affidavit, of the refusal of the collector of customs at the port of St. Andrews, New Brunswick, to allow the master of the American schooner Annie M. Jordan, of Gloucester, Mass., to enter the said vessel at that port, although properly documented as a fishing vessel with permission to touch and trade at any foreign port or place during her voyage.

The object of such entry was explained by the master to be the purchase and exportation of "certain merchandise" (possibly fresh fish for food, or bait for deep-sea fishing).

The vessel was threatened with seizure by the Canadian authorities, and her owners allege that they have sustained damage from this refusal of commercial rights.

I earnestly protest against this unwarranted withholding of lawful commercial privileges from an American vessel and her owners, and for the loss and damage consequent thereon the Government of Great Britain will be held liable.

I have, etc.,
T. F. BAYARD.

How much we shall get will be readily seen when they now meet us at all times with the declarations of the President and the Secretary of State that no such commercial privileges ever existed for our fishing vessels, and that a fishing vessel could not be a fishing vessel and a commercial vessel at the same time.

The Canadian authorities in 1886 warned off all our vessels, threatened them if they did not keep away from that coast. June 14, 1886, Mr. Bayard addressed this letter to Sir Lionel West concerning this matter:

Mr. Bayard to Sir L. West.

DEPARTMENT OF STATE, *Washington, June 14, 1886.*

Sir: The consul-general of the United States at Halifax communicated to me the information derived by him from the collector of customs at that port to the effect that American fishing vessels will not be permitted to land fish at that port of entry for transportation in bond across the province.

I have also to inform you that the masters of the four American fishing vessels of Gloucester, Mass., Martha A. Bradley, Rattler, Eliza Boynton, and Pioneer, have severally reported to the consul-general at Halifax that the subcollector of customs at Canso had warned them to keep outside an imaginary line drawn from a point 3 miles outside Canso Head to a point 3 miles outside St. Esprit, on the Cape Breton coast, a distance of 40 miles. This line for nearly its entire continuance is distant 12 to 25 miles from the coast.

The same masters also report that they were warned against going inside an imaginary line drawn from a point 3 miles outside North Cape, on Prince Edward Island, to a point 3 miles outside of East Point, on the same island, a distance of over 100 miles, and that this last-named line was for nearly that entire distance about 30 miles from the shore.

The same authority informed the masters of the vessels referred to that they would not be permitted to enter Bay Chaleur.

Such warnings are, as you must be well aware, wholly unwarranted pretentions of extraterritorial authority and usurpations of jurisdiction by the provincial officials.

It becomes my duty, in bringing this information to your notice, to request that if any such orders for interference with the unquestionable rights of the American fishermen to pursue their business without molestation at any point not within 3 marine miles of the shores, and within the defined limits as to which renunciation of the liberty to fish was expressed in the treaty of 1818, may have been issued, the same may at once be revoked as violative of the rights of citizens of the United States under convention with Great Britain.

I will ask you to bring this subject to the immediate attention of Her Britannic Majesty's Government, to the end that proper remedial orders may be forthwith issued.

It seems most unfortunate and regretable that questions which have been long since settled between the United States and Great Britain should now be sought to be revived.

I have, etc.,

T. F. BAYARD.

Mr. President, I was not mistaken when I said he had revived the obsolete headland theory. Here is his own statement that it had been abandoned. I will show before I get through that Sir Charles Tupper declared to the Canadian Parliament that it had been abandoned, and every man familiar with the history of these transactions knows that it had been practically abandoned.

Some time in April, 1886, Messrs. Cushing and McKenney, New England men doing business in those waters, addressed a telegram to the Secretary of State seeking to know what their rights were. I have not the telegram here, but the answer is sufficient to show what it was. They asked, "Are we entitled to go in these waters, and what are our rights when we get there?" The reply of the State Department was as follows:

Mr. Bayard to Messrs. Cushing and McKenney.

[Telegram.]

STATE DEPARTMENT, *April 9, 1886.*

The question of the right of American vessels engaged in fishing on the high seas to enter Canadian ports for the purpose of shipping crews may possibly involve construction of treaty with Great Britain. I expect to attain such an understanding as will relieve our fishermen from all doubts or risk in the exercise of the ordinary commercial privileges of friendly ports, to which, under existing laws of both countries, I consider their citizens to be mutually entitled, free from molestation.

T. F. BAYARD.

The Secretary of State expressed his opinion that while it might be difficult to say whether we could ship crews, we could buy bait and we could buy ice and we could buy provisions if the ship was in distress or needed them. Yet to-day we are told that no such rights exist, that they never did exist, and that he who asserts it asserts it simply because he is blind and can not see.

Again, in a letter to Mr. West of May 10, 1886, Mr. Bayard complained of the seizure of vessels as follows, on page 290:

The seizure of the vessels I have mentioned, and certain published "warnings" purporting to have been issued by the colonial authorities, would appear to have been made under a supposeddelegation of jurisdiction by the Imperial Government of Great Britain, and to be intended to include authority to interpret and enforce the provisions of the treaty of 1818, to which, as I have remarked, the United States and Great Britain are the contracting parties, who can alone deal responsibly with questions arising thereunder.

The effect of this colonial legislation and executive interpretation, if executed according to the letter, would be not only to expand the restrictions and renunciations of the treaty of 1818, which related solely to inshore fishery within the 3-mile limit, so as to affect the deep-sea fisheries, the right to which remained unquestioned and unimpaired for the employment of the citizens of the United States, but further to diminish and practically to destroy the privileges expressly secured to American fishing vessels to visit those inshore waters for the objects of shelter, repair of damages, and purchasing wood, and obtaining water.

July 2, 1886, Mr. Bayard complained to Mr. West in the following language:

Mr. Bayard to Sir L. West.

DEPARTMENT OF STATE, *Washington, July 2, 1886.*

SIR: It is my unpleasant duty promptly to communicate to you the telegraphic report to me by the United States consul-general at Halifax, that the schooner City Point, of Portland, Me., arrived at the port of Shelburne, Nova Scotia, landed two men, obtained water, and is detained by the authorities until further instructions are received from Ottawa.

The case as thus reported is an infringement on the ordinary rights of international hospitality, and constitutes a violation of treaty stipulations and commercial privileges, evincing such unfriendliness to the citizens of the United States as is greatly to be deplored, and which I hold it to be the responsible duty of the Government of Great Britain promptly to correct.

I have, etc.,

T. F. BAYARD.

At a later date, July 10, 1886, Mr. Bayard recited another outrage, as follows:

Mr. Bayard to Sir L. West.

DEPARTMENT OF STATE, *Washington, July* 10, 1886.

SIR: I have the honor to inform you that I am in receipt of a report from the consul-general of the United States at Halifax, accompanied by sworn testimony stating that the Novelty, a duly registered merchant steam-vessel of the United States, has been denied the right to take in steam-coal, or purchase ice, or tranship fish in bond to the United States, at Pictou, Nova Scotia.

It appears that, having reached that port on the 1st instant and finding the customs office closed on account of a holiday, the master of the Novelty telegraphed to the minister of marine and fisheries at Ottawa, asking if he would be permitted to do any of the three things mentioned above; that he received in reply a telegram reciting with certain inaccurate and extended application the language of Article I of the treaty of 1818, the limitations upon the significance of which are in pending discussion between the Government of the United States and that of Her Britannic Majesty; that on entering and clearing the Novelty on the following day at the custom-house, the collector stated that his instructions were contained in the telegram the master had received; and that, the privilege of coaling being denied, the Novelty was compelled to leave Pictou without being allowed to obtain fuel necessary for her lawful voyage on a dangerous coast.

Against this treatment I make instant and formal protest as an unwarranted interpretation and application of the treaty by the officers of the Dominion of Canada and the Province of Nova Scotia, as an infraction of the laws of commercial and maritime intercourse existing between the two countries, and as a violation of hospitality, and for any loss or injury resulting therefrom the Government of Her Britannic Majesty will be held liable.

I have, etc.,

T. F. BAYARD.

On the same day, July 10, 1886, Mr. Bayard wrote to Mr. West as follows:

To-day Mr. C. A. BOUTELLE, M. C. from Maine, informs me that American boats visiting St. Andrews, New Brunswick, for the purpose of there purchasing herring from the Canadian weirs, for canning, had been driven away by the Dominion cruiser Middleton.

Such inhibition of usual and legitimate commercial contracts and intercourse is assuredly without warrant of law, and I draw your attention to it in order that the commercial rights of citizens of the United States may not be thus invaded and subjected to unfriendly discrimination.

I have, etc.,

T. F. BAYARD.

July 16, 1886, Mr. Bayard wrote to Mr. Hardinge as follows:

DEPARTMENT OF STATE, *Washington, Ju'y* 16, 1886.

SIR: I have just received through the honorable C. A. BOUTELLE, M. C., the affidavit of Stephen R. Balkam, alleging his expulsion from the harbor of St. Andrews, New Brunswick, by Captain Kent, of the Dominion cruiser Middleton, and the refusal to permit him to purchase fish caught and sold by Canadians, for the purpose of canning as sardines.

The action of Captain Kent seems to be a gross violation of ordinary commercial privileges against an American citizen proposing to transact his customary and lawful trade and not prepared or intending in any way to fish or violate any local law or regulation or treaty stipulation.

I trust instant instructions to prevent the recurrence of such unfriendly and unlawful treatment of American citizens may be given to the offending officials at St. Andrews, and reparation be made to Mr. Balkam.

I have, etc.,

T. F. BAYARD.

Again, July 30, 1886, Mr. Bayard wrote to Sir Lionel West as follows:

DEPARTMENT OF STATE, *Washington, July* 30, 1886.

SIR: It is my duty to draw your attention to an infraction of the stipulations of the treaty between the United States of America and Great Britain, concluded October 20, 1818.

* * * * * * *

I am also in possession of the affidavit of Alexander T. Eachern, master of the American fishing schooner Mascot, who entered Port Amherst, Magdalen Islands, and was there threatened by the customs official with seizure of his vessel if he attempted to obtain bait for fishing or to take a pilot.

These are flagrant violations of treaty rights of their citizens for which the United States expect prompt remedial action by Her Majesty's Government; and I have to ask that such instructions may be issued forthwith to the provincial officials of Newfoundland and of the Magdalen Islands as will cause the treaty rights of citizens of the United States to be duly respected.

For the losses occasioned in the two cases I have mentioned, compensation will hereafter be expected from Her Majesty's Government when the amount shall have been accurately ascertained.

I have, etc.,

T. F. BAYARD.

Later, August 9, 1886, there seems still to have been trouble, and Mr. Bayard addressed Mr. Hardinge, as follows:

Mr. Bayard to Mr. Hardinge.

DEPARTMENT OF STATE, *Washington, August 9, 1896.*

SIR: I regret that it has become my duty to draw the attention of Her Majesty's Government to the unwarrantable and unfriendly treatment, reported to me this day by the United States consul-general at Halifax, experienced by the American fishing schooner Rattler, of Gloucester, Mass., on the 3d instant, upon the occasion of her being driven by stress of weather to find shelter in the harbor of S elburne, Nova Scotia.

*   *   *   *   *   *   *

The vessel was then detained until the captain reported at the custom-house, after which she was permitted to sail.

The hospitality which all civilized nations prescribe has i aus been violated and the stipulations of a treaty grossly infracted.

A fishing vessel, denied all the usual commercial privileges in a port, has been compelled strictly to perform commercial obligations.

In the interests of amity, I ask that this misconduct may be properly rebuked by the government of Her Majesty.

I have, etc.,

T. F. BAYARD.

Later, on August 17, 1886, Mr. Bayard, in a letter to Mr. West, used this language, speaking of another transaction:

I have further the honor to ask with all earnestness that the Government of Her Britannic Majesty will cause steps to be forthwith taken to prevent and rebuke acts so violative of treaty and of the common rites of hospitality.

And on the next day, August 18, 1886, Mr. Bayard, in a letter to the same gentleman, used the following language, speaking of the vessel Rattler:

Such conduct can not be defended on any just ground, and I draw your attention to it in order that Her Britannic Majesty's Government may reprimand Captain Quigley for his unwarranted and rude act.

It was simply impossible for this officer to suppose that any invasion of the fishing privileges of Canada was intended by these vessels under the circumstances.

The firing of a gun across their bows was a most unusual and wholly uncalled for exhibition of hostility, and equally so was the placing of armed men on board the peaceful and lawful craft of a friendly nation.

Speaking of the Molly Adams, in his letter of September 10, 1886, Mr. Bayard said to Mr. West:

This inhospitable, indeed inhuman, conduct on the part of the customs officer in question should be severely reprimanded, and for the infraction of treaty rights and commercial privileges compensation equivalent to the injuries sustained will be claimed from Her Majesty's Government.

Complaining of another transaction, Mr. Bayard, in a letter to Mr. West, said September 23, 1886:

Mr. Bayard to Sir L. West.

DEPARTMENT OF STATE, *Washington, September 23, 1886.*

SIR: I have the honor to bring to your attention an instance which has been brought to my knowledge of an alleged denial of one of the rights guarantied by the convention of 1818, in the case of an American vessel.

Capt. Joseph E. Graham, of the fishing schooner A. R. Crittenden, of Gloucester, Mass., states under oath that on or about the 21st of July last, on a return trip from the open-sea fishing grounds to his home port, and while passing through the Strait of Canso, he stopped at Steep Creek for water. The customs officer at that place told him that if he took in water his vessel would be seized;

whereupon he sailed without obtaining the needed supply, and was obliged to put his men on short allowance of water during the passage homeward.

I have the honor to ask that Her Britannic Majesty's Government cause investigation to be made of the reported action of the customs officer at Steep Creek, and if the facts be as stated, that he be promptly rebuked for his unlawful and inhumane conduct in denying to a vessel of a friendly nation a general privilege, which is not only held sacred under the maritime law of nations, but which is expressly confirmed to the fishermen of the United States throughout the Atlantic coasts of British North America by the first article of the convention of 1818.

It does not appear that the A. R. Crittenden suffered other damage by this alleged inhospitable treatment, but reserving that point the incident affords an illustration of the vexatious spirit in which the officers of the Dominion of Canada appear to seek to penalize and oppress those fishing vessels of the United States, lawfully engaged in fishing, which from any cause are brought within their reach.

I have, etc.,

T. F. BAYARD.

I shall not encumber the RECORD by putting in all these letters. Suffice it to say that up to the time these negotiations began, the Secretary of State on and off, again and again, declared that the Canadian authorities 'were violating the treaty, and not only violating the treaty but violating the common courtesies that were due from one friendly nation to another. Not only did he so assert to the British Government, but he instructed our minister at London to so assert, and he did so assert on various occasions. As suggested by the Senator from Connecticut [Mr. PLATT], he did that to American citizens who were demanding to know what their rights were, that they might not be led into a trap. He said: "Your rights are to go in there and buy." Now he asserts that no such right ever existed. When did he get the new light?

In a letter to Mr. Phelps on November 6, 1886, Mr. Bayard asserted this same right and directed him to assert it. He said, on page 437:

From Her Majesty's Government redress is asked. And that redress, as I shall have occasion to say hereafter, is not merely the indemnification of the parties suffering by Captain Quigley's actions, but his withdrawal from the waters where the outrages I represent to you have been committed.

I have already said that the claims thus presented could be abundantly sustained by the law of nations, aside from treaty and other rights. But I am not willing to rest the case on the law of nations. It is essential that the issue between United States fishing vessels and the "cruiser Terror" should be examined in all its bearings, and settled in regard not merely to the general law of nations, but to the particular rights of the parties aggrieved.

It is a fact that the fishing vessel Marion Grimes had as much right under the special relations of Great Britain and the United States to enter the harbor of Shelburne as had the Canadian cruiser. The fact that the Grimes was liable to penalties for the abuse of such right of entrance does not disprove its existence. Captain Quigley is certainly liable to penalties for his misconduct on the occasion referred to. Captain Landry was not guilty of misconduct in entering and seeking to leave that harbor, and had abused no privilege. But whether liable or not for subsequent abuse of the rights, I maintain that the right of free entrance into that port to obtain shelter, and whatever is incident thereto, belonged as much to the American fishing vessel as to the Canadian cruiser.

The basis of this right is thus declared by an eminent jurist and statesman, Mr. R. R. Livingston, the first Secretary of State appointed by the Continental Congress, in instructions issued on January 7, 1782, to Dr. Franklin, then at Paris, intrusted by the United States with the negotiation of articles of peace with Great Britain:

"The arguments on which the people of America found their claim to fish on the banks of Newfoundland arise, first, from their having once formed a part of the British Empire, in which state they always enjoyed as fully as the people of Britain themselves the right of fishing on those banks. They have shared in all the wars for the extension of that right, and Britain could with no more justice have excluded them from the enjoyment of it (even supposing that one nation could possess it to the exclusion of another) while they formed a part of that empire than they could exclude the people of London or Bristol.

"If so, the only inquiry is, how have we lost this right? If we were tenants in common with Great Britain while united with her, we still continue so, unless by our own act we have relinquished our title. Had we parted with mutual consent, we should doubtless have made partition of our common rights by treaty. But the oppressions of Great Britain forced us to a separation (which must be admitted, or we have no right to be independent); and it can not certainly be contended that those oppressions abridged our rights or gave new ones to Britain. Our rights, then, are not invalidated by this separation, more particularly as we have kept up our claim from the commencement of the war, and assigned the attempt of Great Britain to exclude us from the fisheries as one of the causes of our recurring to arms."

* * * * * * *

At present it is sufficient to say that the placing an armed cruiser at the mouth of a harbor in which the United States fishing vessels are accustomed and are entitled to seek shelter on their voyages, such cruiser being authorized to arrest and board our fishing vessels seeking such shelter, is an infraction not merely of the law of nations, but of a solemn treaty stipulation. That, so far as concerns the fishermen so affected, its consequences are far-reaching and destructive, it is not necessary here to argue. Fishing vessels only carry provisions enough for each particular voyage. If they are detained several days on their way to the fishing banks, the venture is broken up. The arrest and detention of one or two operates upon all. They can not, as a class, with their limited capital and resources, afford to run risks so ruinous.

Hence, rather than subject themselves to even the chances of suffering the wrongs inflicted by Captain Quigley, "of the Canadian cruiser Terror," on some of their associates, they might prefer to abandon their just claim to the shelter consecrated to them alike by humanity, ancient title, the law of nations, and by treaty, and face the gravest peril and the wildest seas in order to reach their fishing grounds. You will therefore represent to Her Majesty's Government that the placing Captain Quigley in the harbor of Shelburne to inflict wrongs and humiliation on United States fishermen there seeking shelter is, in connection with other methods of annoyance and injury, expelling United States fishermen from waters, access to which, of great importance in the pursuit of their trade, is pledged to them by Great Britain, not merely as an ancient right, but as part of a system of international settlement.

Here I should like to say that I have gone carefully over the correspondence of the American minister, Mr. Phelps, and I believe that he presented the case with great force. I do not know whether he has changed base, too. I do not know whether he will now be the apologist, like the Secretary of State and the Democratic Senate, of the Canadian officials; but I know that from time to time he asserted in language, as I have before said, verging to the extreme of diplomatic courtesy, that these transactions were without authority of law and were violative of the treaty. He said to Lord Iddesleigh, September 11, 1886:

To two recent instances of interference by Canadian officers with American fishermen, of a somewhat different character, I am specially instructed by my Government to ask your lordship's attention, those of the schooners Thomas F. Bayard and Mascot.

These vessels were proposing to fish in waters in which the right to fish is expressly secured to Americans by the terms of the treaty of 1818; the former in Bonne Bay, on the northwest coast of Newfoundland, and the latter near the shores of the Magdalen Islands.

For this purpose the Bayard attempted to purchase bait in the port of Bonne Bay, having reported at the custom-house and announced its object. The Mascot made a similar attempt at Port Amherst in the Magdalen Islands, and also desired to take on board a pilot. Both vessels were refused permission by the authorities to purchase bait, and the Mascot to take a pilot, and were notified to leave the ports within twenty-four hours on penalty of seizure. They were therefore compelled to depart, to break up their voyages, and to return home, to their very great loss. I append copies of the affidavits of the masters of these vessels stating the facts.

Your lordship will observe, upon reference to the treaty, not only that the right to fish in these waters is conferred by it, but that the clause prohibiting entry by American fishermen into Canadian ports, except for certain specified purposes, which is relied on by the Canadian Government in the cases of the Adams and of some other vessels, has no application whatever to the ports from which the Bayard and the Mascot were excluded. The only prohibition in the treaty having reference to those ports is against curing and drying fish there, without leave of the inhabitants, which the vessels excluded had no intention of doing.

The conduct of the provincial officers toward these vessels was therefore not merely unfriendly and injurious, but in clear and plain violation of the terms of the treaty. And I am instructed to say that reparation for the losses sustained by it to the owners of the vessels will be claimed by the United States Government on their behalf as soon as the amount can be accurately ascertained.

There are several letters from this minister of the same character asserting that our fishermen had rights there.

Mr. President, these assertions are in harmony with the construction given to the treaty of 1818 by the British Government themselves from time to time. I propose briefly to call the attention of the Senate to this point. I submit the letter of Mr. Phelps to Lord Roseberry of June 2, 1886, page 415, in which he details particularly the cases wherein the British Government had surrendered the headland theory and the right to exclude our fishermen from the bays.

*   *   *   *   *   *

The British Government has repeatedly refused to allow interference with American fishing vessels, unless for illegal fishing, and has given explicit orders to the contrary.

On the 26th of May, 1870, Mr. Thornton, the British minister at Washington, communicated officially to the Secretary of State of the United States copies of the orders addressed by the British Admiralty to Admiral Wellesley, commanding Her Majesty's naval forces on the North American station, and of a letter from the colonial department to the foreign office, in order that the Secretary might "see the nature of the instructions to be given to Her Majesty's and the Canadian officers employed in maintaining order at the fisheries in the neighborhood of the coasts of Canada." Among the documents thus transmitted is a letter from the foreign office to the secretary of the Admiralty, in which the following language is contained:

"The Canadian Government has recently determined, with the concurrence of Her Majesty's ministers, to increase the stringency of the existing practice of dispensing with the warnings hitherto given, and seizing at once any vessel detected in violation of the law.

"In view of this change and of the questions to which it may give rise, I am directed by Lord Granville to request that you will move their lordships to instruct the officers of Her Majesty's ships employed in the protection of the fisheries that they are not to seize any vessel unless it is evident and can be clearly proved that the offense of fishing has been committed and the vessel itself captured within 3 miles of land."

In the letter from the lords of the Admiralty to Vice-Admiral Wellesley of May 5, 1870, in accordance with the forego'ng request, and transmitting the letter above quoted from, there occurs the following language:

"My lords desire me to remind you of the extreme importance of commanding officers of the ships selected to protect the fisheries exercising the utmost discretion in carrying out their instructions, paying special attention to Lord Granville's observation that no vessel should be seized unless it is evident and can be clearly proved that the offense of fishing has been committed and that the vessel is captured within 3 miles of land."

Lord Granville, in transmitting to Sir John Young the aforesaid instructions, makes use of the following language:

"Her Majesty's Government do not doubt that your ministers will agree with them as to the propriety of these instructions, and will give corresponding instructions to the vessels employed by them."

These instructions were again officially stated by the British minister at Washington to the Secretary of State of the United States in a letter dated June 11, 1870.

Again, in February, 1871, Lord Kimberly, colonial secretary, wrote to the governor-general of Canada as follows:

"The exclusion of American fishermen from resorting to Canadian ports, except for the purpose of shelter, and of repairing damages therein, purchasing wood, and of obtaining water, might be warranted by the letter of the treaty of 1818, and by the terms of the imperial act 59 George III, chapter 38, but Her Majesty's Government feel bound to state that it seems to them an extreme measure, inconsistent with the general policy of the empire, and they are disposed to concede this point to the United States Government under such restrictions as may be necessary to prevent smuggling, and to guard against any substantial invasion of the exclusive rights of fishing which may be reserved to British subjects."

And in a subsequent letter from the same source to the governor-general, the following language is used:

"I think it right, however, to add that the responsibility of determining what is the true construction of a treaty made by Her Majesty with any foreign power

32

must remain with Her Majesty's Government, and that the degree to which this country would make itself a party to the strict enforcement of the treaty rights may depend not only on the literal construction of the treaty, but on the moderation and reasonableness with which these rights are asserted."

I am not aware that any modification of these instructions or any different rule from that therein contained has ever been adopted or sanctioned by Her Majesty's Government.

Judicial authority upon this question is to the same effect. That the purchase of bait by American fishermen in the provincial ports has been a common practice is well known. But in no case, so far as I can ascertain, has a seizure of an American vessel ever been enforced on the ground of the purchase of bait, or of any other supplies. On the hearing before the Halifax Fisheries Commission in 1877 this question was discussed, and no case could be produced of any such condemnation. Vessels shown to have been condemned were in all cases adjudged guilty, either of fishing, or preparing to fish, within the prohibited limit. And in the case of the White Fawn, tried in the admiralty court of New Brunswick before Judge Hazen in 1870, I understand it to have been distinctly held that the purchase of bait, unless proved to have been in preparation for illegal fishing, was not a violation of the treaty, nor of any existing law, and afforded no ground for proceedings against the vessel.

I also submit a paper found in Executive Document No. 113, marked Appendix B, showing the construction put upon the treaty by the British authorities:

APPENDIX B.

In such capacity your jurisdiction must be strictly confined within the limits of "3 marine miles of any of the coasts, bays, creeks, or harbors" of Canada, with respect to any action you may take against American fishing vessels and United States citizens engaged in fishing. Where any of the bays, creeks, or harbors shall not exceed 6 geographical miles in width, you will consider that the line of demarcation extends from headland to headland, either at the entrance to such bay, creek, or harbor, or from and between given points on both sides thereof, at any place nearest the mouth where the shores are less than 6 miles apart; and may exclude foreign fishermen and fishing vessels therefrom, or seize if found within 3 marine miles of the coast.

Jurisdiction.—The limits within which you will, if necessary, exercise the power to exclude the United States fishermen, or to detain American fishing vessels or boats, are for the present to be exceptional. Difficulties have arisen in former times with respect to the question whether the exclusive limits should be measured on lines drawn parallel everywhere to the coast and describing its sinuosities, or on lines produced from headland to headland across the entrances of bays, creeks, or harbors. Her Majesty's Government are clearly of opinion that by the convention of 1818 the United States have renounced the right of fishing not only within 3 miles of the colonial shores, but within 3 miles of a line drawn across the mouth of any British bay or creek.

It is, however, the wish of Her Majesty's Government neither to concede, nor for the present to enforce any rights in this respect which are in their nature open to any serious question. Until further instructed, therefore, you will not interfere with any American fishermen unless found within 3 miles of the shore, or within 3 miles of a line drawn across the mouth of a bay or a creek which, though in parts more than 6 miles wide, is less than 6 geographical miles in width at its mouth. In the case of any other bay, as the Bay des Chaleurs for example, you will not interfere with any United States fishing vessel or boat, or any American fishermen, unless they are found within 3 miles of the shore.

"Action.—You will accost every United States vessel or boat actually within 3 marine miles of the shore along any other part of the coast except Labrador and around the Magdalen Islands, or within 3 marine miles of the entrance of any bay, harbor, or creek which is less than 6 geographical miles in width, or inside of a line drawn across any part of such bay harbor, or creek at points nearest to the mouth thereof not wider apart than 6 geographical miles, and if either fishing, preparing to fish, or having obviously fished within the exclusive limits, you will, in accordance with the above-recited acts, seize at once any vessel detected in violating the law, and send or take her into port for condemnation; but you are not to do so unless it is evident, and can be clearly proved, that the offense of fishing has been committed, and that the vessel is captured within the prohibited limits." (Session Papers, volume IV, No. 4, 1871.)

APPENDIX C.—The secretary of state for the colonies to the governor-general.

DOWNING STREET, October 10, 1870.

SIR: I inclose a copy of a memorandum, which I have requested Lord Granville to transmit to Sir E. Thornton, with instructions to communicate with you before addressing himself to the Government of United States on the subject to which the memorandum relates.

The object of Her Majesty's Government is, as you will observe, to give effect to the wishes of your Government, by appointing a joint commission, on which Great Britain, the United States, and Canada are to be represented, with the object of inquiring what ought to be the geographical limits of the exclusive fisheries of the British North American colonies. In accordance with the understood desire of your advisers it is proposed that the inquiry should be held in America.

The proposal contained in the last paragraph is made with a view to avoid diplomatic difficulties, which might otherwise attend the negotiation.

I have, etc.,

KIMBERLY.

Governor-General the Right Hon. Sir JOHN YOUNG, G. C. B., G. C. M. G.

We have both Houses of Congress and we have the Department of State in favor of our construction of the treaty of 1818. We have in addition to that the fact that the claim either to exclude us from bays or from lines drawn from headland to headland was not set up for many years after; that it was referred to by Secretary Everett in 1843 as a new claim made by the Canadians, and then not made by the British. We have all these things to justify us in insisting that the construction put upon the treaty by our predecessors is correct.

I think that is a sufficient answer to the Senators who have accused us of partisanship and a desire to antagonize this Administration, as well as a reply to the undignified interview in which the Secretary of State recently said, if the Baltimore Sun correctly reports him, that the Republican Senators were actuated only by a desire to embarrass the Administration. There is not a position that we have taken on this subject which has not been taken by the Secretary of State himself. There is not a position that we have taken on the treaty of 1818 that has not been taken by his minister to Great Britain.

What do Senators on the other side say? Do they suppose that the Secretary of State and the American minister were simply making a claim that they in truth knew did not in fact exist, or have they seen a new light under the manipulation or the advice of Sir Ambrose Shea, Joseph Chamberlain, and Sir Lionel West?

I said I would not take time to discuss the headland theory. It has been abandoned by Great Britain practically for years. It is abandoned now, or would have been but for this treaty. Mr. Tupper in discussing this question before the Canadian Parliament admitted that it had been abandoned.

So I think I may come to the treaty itself, and see whether there is anything in the treaty that is an improvement on the existing order of things.

I do not desire to go into any discussion of the right of the Secretary of State, or of the President, more properly speaking, to initiate this proceeding. I say that it was a most remarkable transaction, and I think it has no precedent in history, with the Senate of the United States about to convene, within ten days of its session, that the President should select a commission which should sit here for months during the session, and that he should not send in their names to the Senate for confirmation. But if the treaty was a good treaty, one commending itself to the American people and the American Senate, I should be in favor of waiving all these irregularities and of taking the treaty as it is. But such is not the case.

In the first place, we ought not to treat with Great Britain at all at this time. Such was almost the unanimous sense of the American Senate. It would have been unanimously held a year later, had the question been submitted, that we ought not to treat at all with all these outrages unredressed, with our ships boarded, taken into port, fined, hindered, injured, ruined in their business, and further, the American flag pulled down and insulted. Yet that has been done without an apology worthy of the name for these insults to the flag and the nation. We are asked to treat with Great Britain upon this question, to surrender that which was incontestably ours, as I intend to show when I take up the treaty in detail. We have under this proposed treaty nothing that we did not have without it. We have no opportunity for redress for the wrongs inflicted. We have, it is true, for the lowering of the flag what they call an apology.

Mr. President, I wish to say a word on that point, because on two or three occasions when this question has been up it has been said that Great Britain has apologized. I assert that Great Britain has never indicated the slightest compunction as to the Canadian conduct, and I do not know that Great Britain supposes she is liable for anything. Yet we do not deal with Canada. If an apology came at all, it should come from Great Britain. But let us hear what kind of an apology we got. I remember a year ago and more, when this matter was under discussion, the Senator from Missouri [Mr. VEST] said that there had been an apology. The Senator from Maryland [Mr. GORMAN], who was discussing the question a little later, said that there had been an apology, but he said it was a very unsatisfactory apology. I say it was no apology at all. Let us hear what they said:

WASHINGTON, *December 7, 1886.*

SIR: I am instructed by the Earl of Iddesleigh to communicate to you the inclosed copy of a dispatch, with its inclosures, from the officer administering the Government of Canada, expressing the regret of the Dominion Government at the action of the captain of the Canadian cutter Terror in lowering the United States flag from the United States fishing schooner Marion Grimes, of Gloucester, Mass., while that vessel was under detention at Shelburne, Nova Scotia.
I have, etc.,

L. S. SACKVILLE WEST.

Here is the inclosure:

Acting Governor Lord A. G. Russell to Mr. Stanhope.

HALIFAX, NOVA SCOTIA, *October 27, 1886.*

SIR: I have the honor to transmit herewith a copy of an approved minute of the privy council of Canada, expressing the regret of my Government at the action of the captain of the Canadian cutter Terror in lowering the United States flag from the United States fishing schooner Marion Grimes, of Gloucester, Mass., while that vessel was under detention at Shelburne, Nova Scotia, by the collector of customs at that port for an infraction of the customs regulations.
I have communicated a copy of this order in council to Her Majesty's minister at Washington.
I have, etc.,

A. G. RUSSELL, *General.*

This is the next inclosure:

[Inclosure 2 in No. 57.]

Report of a committee of the honorable the privy council for Canada, approved by his excellency the administrator of the Government in council on the 20th October, 1886.

On a report, dated the 14th October, 1886, from Hon. Mackenzie Bowell, for the minister of marine and fisheries, stating that on Monday, the 11th October instant, the United States fishing schooner Marion Grimes, of Gloucester, Mass., was under detention at Shelburne, Nova Scotia, by the collector of customs at that port for an infraction of the customs regulations; that while so detained, and under the surveillance of the Canadian Government cutter Terror, the captain of the Marion Grimes hoisted the United States flag.

The minister further states that it appears that Captain Quigley, of the Terror, considered such act as an intimation that there was an intention to rescue the vessel, and requested Captain Landry to take the flag down. This request was complied with. An hour later, however, the flag was again hoisted, and on Captain Landry being asked if his vessel had been released, and replying that she had not, Captain Quigley again requested that the flag be lowered. This was refused, when Captain Quigley himself lowered the flag, acting under the belief that while the Marion Grimes was in possession of the customs authorities, and until her case had been adjudicated upon, the vessel had no right to fly the United States flag.

Now, here is the apology, Mr. President.

The minister regrets that he should have acted with undue zeal, although Captain Quigley may have been technically within his right while the vessel was in the custody of the law.

The committee advise that your excellency be moved to forward a copy of this minute, if approved, to the right honorable the secretary of state for the colonies, and to Her Majesty's minister at Washington, expressing the regret of the Canadian Government at the occurrence.

All of which is respectfully submitted for your excellency's approval.
JOHN J. McGEE,
Clerk, Privy Council.

Mr. President, I assert that no international lawyer in the Senate or anywhere will stand up and claim that before adjudication there is any right in the Government seizing a vessel to take down its flag. It is a universal law of the world that the flag flies until the adjudication determines the question of the right of seizure. So there Canadian authorities simply regretted that Captain Quigley acted with undue zeal, and then asserted the right to pull down the American flag whenever they seized a vessel, and it is only a question with them of policy and not a question of law.

The State Department knew that that was not the international law, for the Secretary of State himself, in one of his letters to Mr. Phelps, declares that the Canadians had no right to take down the flag until it was determined there was a rightful and proper seizure of the vessel.

Mr. President, how long do you think they would have been without an apology of a proper kind if we had pulled down the British flag floating over a Canadian fisherman? How long do you think it would have been before we should have been notified that we were to disavow the act of that officer or to make an humble apology?

Great Britain does not proceed in that way when her flag is insulted. She does not wait. Neither have we been wont to wait when the American flag was assailed. It is left for this Administration to accept an apology which says, "We had a right to take down your flag; you ought not to complain; we think it was a little undue zeal on the part of our officer, and yet the right exists." Out upon such an apology, Mr. President! It ought to make every American ashamed, and it does. I know that there are men in the Democratic party who are ashamed of it. I am sorry to say that they seem to have lost the courage to say what they must think, and what all honest, upright, brave people must think of such a transaction.

Once upon an occasion an overzealous United States naval officer seized two Confederate messengers going abroad. You may remember it. It was in the fall of 1861. He seized a British ship because it was carrying contraband passengers, but instead of complying with the law of nations and bringing in the ship, he let the ship go and took out of it the men, and thus put himself beyond the pale of international law. What did the British Government do with us then? They gave us notice that we should return those men to British control and authority inside of seven days or there would be war. They did not wait seven days before they started by the quickest transportation in their power their troops to the Canadian provinces.

There is not a man here who does not know that there is not any nation in the world who would dare to do such a thing to Great Britain; and are they to get off with an apology of the character I have read?

I do not wonder that the Senator from Maryland said that it was not a satisfactory apology.

But, Mr. President, it is in keeping with the whole course of this Administration on this question. It is in keeping with the whole course of the Administration in its dealings with the British Government. I can not assume that the Administration was afraid to demand a sufficient apology. I must assume that the Administration is not sufficiently alive to indignities inflicted upon this country. That is the excuse, and that probably is the only one. If it had been sufficiently alive to the wrongs inflicted no treaty would have been made, no negotiation would have been entered into until there had been some redress at least promised for all the wrongs inflicted upon us by the Canadian officials.

I desire to call the attention of the Senate briefly to some provisions of the new treaty and then I shall not detain the Senate longer upon this subject. The treaty comes here with the President's approval. The Senator from Delaware [Mr. GRAY] says it comes with great presumptive weight. He says that a treaty always comes with great presumptive weight from an administration, and it always has it. Time and again a Republican administration has sent to a Republican Senate treaties which have been rejected, and rejected, too, by Republican votes. When was it that the American Senate became subordinate to the executive department in considering these subjects and determining what treaties ought and what ought not to be ratified? With great presumptive weight! The President, after detailing the treaty, says:

The treaty meets my approval, because I believe that it supplies a satisfactory, practical, and final adjustment, upon a basis honorable and just to both parties, of the difficult and vexed question to which it relates.

A review of the history of this question will show that all former attempts to arrive at a common interpretation, satisfactory to both parties, of the first article of the treaty of October 20, 1818, have been unsuccessful; and with the lapse of time the difficulty and obscurity have only increased.

*   *   *   *   *   *   *

But I believe the treaty will be found to contain a just, honorable, and therefore satisfactory solution of the difficulties which have clouded our relations with our neighbors on our northern border.

Especially satisfactory do I believe the proposed arrangement will be found by those of our citizens who are engaged in the open-sea fisheries, adjacent to the Canadian coast, and resorting to those ports and harbors under the treaty provisions and rules of international law.

The proposed delimitation of the lines of the exclusive fisheries from the common fisheries will give certainty and security as to the area of their legitimate field; the headland theory of imaginary lines is abandoned by Great Britain, and the specifications in the treaty of certain named bays especially provided for gives satisfaction to the inhabitants of the shores, without subtracting materially from the value or convenience of the fishery rights of Americans.

The uninterrupted navigation of the Strait of Canso is expressly and for the first time affirmed.

I shall show that the President could not have read the treaty with care or he would not have made that assertion—

and the four purposes for which our fishermen under the treaty of 1818 were allowed to enter the bays and harbors of Canada and Newfoundland within the belt of 3 marine miles are placed under a fair and liberal construction, and their enjoyment secured without such conditions and restrictions as in the past have embarrassed and obstructed them so seriously.

I do not wonder that Mr. Tupper pointed to this and said with great glee, "What will that do for us when we come to negotiate again?" Here is the President of the United States telling the whole world that our interpretation of the treaty is a fair, honorable, and just one; and that the treaty is all that the Americans can expect. Then the President follows with his explanations. Now, let us s e what the President says about the commercial rights that the Secretary of State had declared to American citizens existed, and which they had been encouraged to assert under this Administration:

The right of our fishermen under the treaty of 1818 did not extend to the procurement of distinctive fishery supplies in Canadian ports and harbors; and one item, supposed to be essential, to wit, bait, was plainly denied them by the explicit and definite words of the treaty of 1818, emphasized by the course of the negotiation and express decisions which preceded the conclusion of that treaty.

Who is at fault, the President of the United States or the Secretary of State? Both can not be right.

I now desire to briefly call attention to the proposed treaty itself. I shall speak of only one or two sections to any extent, and I shall not dwell very much on those.

In brief, the treaty provides for a commission, two commissioners to be selected by the Government of the United States, and two to be selected by the British Government, and in case of a disagreement an umpire to be selected. These commissioners are to be appointed for the purpose of delimiting the several bays. Without, however, waiting for that, the treaty proposes that the delimitation shall be made in the manner described, and then proceeds to make some of the delimitations without waiting for the commission.

The delimitation shall be made in the following manner, and shall be accepted by both the high contracting parties as applicable for all purposes under Article I of the convention of October 20, 1818, between the United States and Great Britain.

The 3 marine miles mentioned in Article I of the convention of October 20, 1818, shall be measured seaward from low-water mark; but at every bay, creek, or harbor, not otherwise specially provided for in this treaty, such 3 marine miles shall be measured seaward from a straight line drawn across the bay, creek, or harbor, in the part nearest the entrance at the first point where the width does not exceed 10 miles.

The Senator from Delaware went into an extended argument to show that 3 marine miles was not the present international law, and the Senator from Mississippi [Mr. GEORGE] went into an extended argument to show that the British owned all the country up there, and therefore allowing us to come within the 10 miles was quite a favor.

It is not necessary for us to consider what the international law is upon this subject. We had a treaty. We had fixed 3 miles. That had received its construction, which was, that the smaller bays that were 6 miles or less were included in the prohibited waters; but now bays that are 10 miles wide are to be included in the prohibited waters. Bays that are much wider than that are prohibited by the delimitation in this treaty, and yet the President of the United States says that these delimitations "will give certainty and security" to the people of the United States who want to fish in those waters.

The proposed delimitation of the lines of the exclusive fisheries from the common fisheries will give certainty and security as to the area of their legitimate field.

Mr. President, is that possible? How can a fisherman see who is to keep outside of 3 miles, the line drawn from another invisible line that is 10 miles long, being more than 6 or 8 miles out from shore, and how can it benefit him any to have these delimitations? It only opens the door for more difficulty and more confusion and more trouble on the part of the fisherman. What he could see and might escape before, he can not see now and can not escape. To say nothing of the great surrender of a large area of fishing ground that is rightfully ours, we are adding to the embarrassment of every man who goes into those waters to fish by lengthening the line so as to keep him from the shore, making it more difficult for him to determine where he is.

Then follow, in Article IV, the bays which are delimited, of which I have not time to speak at any length. Then comes Article V:

ARTICLE V.

Nothing in this treaty shall be construed to include within the common waters any such interior portions of any bays, creeks, or harbors as can not be reached from the sea without passing within the 3 marine miles mentioned in Article I of the convention of October 20, 1818.

I wish to call the attention of the Senate to what Sir Charles Tupper says about that, and why he says that was put in. Mr. Mills, of Both-well, asked him why this provision was inserted, and he said:

Sir CHARLES TUPPER. I am obliged to my honorable friend for his question, and I will give him a most explicit and, I am quite sure, a satisfactory answer. I hold the delineation of a bay in my hands. It is imaginary, it is true, but it is none the less just what you may meet with at the mouth of any bay. This bay is 15 miles from mainland to mainland, and yet under the instructions of my honorable friend from Northumberland [Mr. Mitchell] not to go within 3 miles of the shore they could not get into that bay. Why? Because there are islands in the mouth of the bay, and the island carries its 3 miles of marine jurisdiction stretched around it, the same as the mainland. I will send it over to my honorable friend to show him just what that article means, and the reason why it was necessary, in order to provide for a possible contingency by which a bay being 15 miles wide they could not get into it now. I said: You do not propose by that 10-mile arrangement to enter a bay that you could not enter under the 6-mile arrangement, do you? Certainly not. Then I gave them this delineation, and that clause was put in the treaty for the purpose of giving effect to it, and to prevent giving any possible uncertainty. Now, sir, as I said before, we were met in a broad and liberal spirit, and I think the sentiment that animated us on both sides was that we owed it to each other and to the countries we represented not to quarrel over points that could be satisfactorily adjusted.

That was put in there, it seems, for the benefit of the Canadians, and not for us.

I do not care to look at the other articles, except Article IX, which refers to the Strait of Canso.

ARTICLE IX.

Nothing in this treaty shall interrupt or affect the free navigation of the Strait of Canso by fishing vessels of the United States.

The President of the United States declares in his message to Congress that this guaranties to us some rights that we did not have before. It has simply said as to the Strait of Canso that it leaves it right where it is. Any claim that the British Government ever made to that strait they can make to-day notwithstanding this treaty. What claims they have made in the past I do not care at this late hour to undertake to cite, and I shall not speak of the character of their claims.

We come now to Article X, which is supposed to have great merit. It was much dwelt on by some of the Senators who have discussed this question. It provides, speaking of our vessels, that—

They need not report, enter, or clear, when putting into such bays or harbors for shelter or repairing damages, nor when putting into the same, outside the limits of established ports of entry, for the purpose of purchasing wood or obtaining water; except that any such vessel remaining more than twenty-four hours, exclusive of Sundays and legal holidays, within any such port, or communicating with the shore therein, may be required to report, enter, or clear; and no vessel shall be excused hereby from giving due information to boarding officers. * * *

Mr. President, is there very much in that? Is there very much in the provision that they need enter and clear except under certain circumstances? Mr. Tupper says that if they communicate with the shore for any purpose they must enter and clear. Mr. Tupper said that he did not think it was worth while to insist upon their entering and clearing; that we did not do that with the British vessels which came into our ports under like circumstances; and he said they took the testimony of one of the oldest collectors in the country, the collector of the port of Portland, who asserted that for thirty years he had never known a vessel to be disturbed for remaining more than twenty-four hours without entering and clearing. Whatever might be the statute which was recited by the Senator from Delaware, it has been a dead letter as applied to Canadian vessels. If the fisherman communicates with the shore to get wood, or water, or a doctor, or for any other purpose whatever, he must enter and clear. There is no concession there at all. That is the very extent that any nation requires of people coming into its ports. This article refers to those who come for shelter and repairing damages, for the purchase of wood, or to obtain water, and then they need not, unless they communicate, and as they must communicate it amounts to saying that they shall enter and clear.

Article X also provides that—

They shall not be liable in any such bays or harbors for compulsory pilotage.

Mr. Tupper said that the Canadian fishermen were not subject to that in American ports, and I understand that to be the rule. They are not in New England. The Senator from Massachusetts [Mr. Hoar] thinks they are perhaps in some of the Southern ports. Perhaps there was a reservation some years ago in a statute to that effect. However, I think Mr. Tupper made the statement that there were no compulsory pilotage dues exacted here. I have a reference to it.

Article XI is claimed to have great merit, and to be a very great concession by the Canadian Government to us. It is one of the strong points in this treaty; it is one of the things on account of which it is urged upon our attention. That article provides:

United States fishing vessels entering the ports, bays, and harbors of the eastern and northeastern coasts of Canada, or of the coasts of Newfoundland under stress of weather or other casualty, may unload, reload, transship, or sell, subject to customs laws and regulations, all fish on board, when such unloading, transshipment, or sale is made necessary as incidental to repairs, and may replenish outfits, provisions, and supplies damaged or lost by disaster; and in case of death or sickness shall be allowed all needful facilities, including the shipping of crews.

In 1794, when we were denied commercial relations with Great Britain, not only in Canada, but in all British colonies, we made a treaty with Great Britain which contained stipulations of greater value than this. The stipulation then was not only that we might do all that is now proposed to be done, but we might go further and barter our merchandise for such things as we needed.

There is nothing in this provision of the treaty, as Mr. Tupper says. He says the Canadian Government ought to be ashamed to deny to any foreigners the privileges that are conceded here, not the privileges conceded here as claimed by the Senator from Delaware, not the privileges conceded if the President and Secretary of State are correct, but according to his interpretation, which is in accordance with the interpretation put upon it by the Senator from Massachusetts [Mr. Hoar] the other day when he addressed the Senate.

The article refers only to vessels that go in there under stress of weather or other casualty, and when they so go in they may do what? Unload, reload, transship, or sell, subject to customs laws and regulations? Oh, no, not that. They may do all that when such unloading, transshipment, or sale is necessary as incidental to repairs. When they are in such distress that they can not keep their cargo afloat in their vessels, then they may apply to the British authorities, and if the British authorities think it is a case of distress, of casualty, they may be allowed to ship, provided they show that it is necessary as incidental to repairs. If they can not make their repairs without it, then they may do it. It is a barren right. It is of no earthly account, and was not intended to be. ·

"In case of death or sickness" they shall have "all needful facilities, including the shipping of crews." All this is dependent, first, upon the fact that they are driven in by stress of weather; then that the Canadian authorities think it is incidental to repairs, or that it is necessary. With the disposition that the Canadian authorities have shown toward our fishermen for the last few years, how much benefit do you suppose our fishermen will derive under that provision of the treaty?

There is another clause in Article XI which the Senator from Delaware insisted was an unrestricted license to trade by fishermen, or that at least was the theory upon which he went.

Licenses to purchase in established ports of entry of the aforesaid coasts of Canada or of Newfoundland, for the homeward voyage, such provisions and supplies as are ordinarily sold to trading vessels, shall be granted to United States fishing vessels in such ports, promptly upon application and without charge; and such vessels having obtained licenses in the manner aforesaid shall also be accorded upon all occasions such facilities for the purchase of casual or needful provisions and supplies as are ordinarily granted to the trading vessels; but such provisions or supplies shall not be obtained by barter, nor purchased for resale or traffic.

The Senator from Delaware insisted the other day that this was an unlimited right to purchase for the homeward voyage such provisions as were ordinarily sold to trading vessels. This license only applies to vessels that have gone into these ports in stress of weather. It only applies to such vessels as go there because they could not keep out, to such vessels as come in in distress or by reason of some disaster that has occurred or will occur if they stay out. It is only to that class of vessels that this license is granted.

Then what are they to buy? For the homeward voyage only. If they come in in the beginning of their fishing season, before they have had time to fish and get ready to return, and if they meet disaster and lose a portion of their supplies, they can not go in and buy. It is only when they can satisfy the Canadian Government that they are on the homeward move, and that they will starve to death, as suggested by the Senator from Connecticut [Mr. PLATT], before they get home if they can not buy.

Between two great nations speaking the same language, having so many things in common, do we need a treaty for things like that? Can Great Britain afford to deny to the distressed fishermen of this country or any other that come into her ports the right to purchase supplies to take them home? There is no nation to-day on earth that denies that to the distressed mariner. Yet that provision is put in this treaty and it is held up to us as a great merit, one which we should surrender almost anything to secure, and because we do not see it in that light we are moved wholly and solely by partisan zeal and by a desire to embarrass the Administration!

I said that Mr. Tupper did not entertain the same views about this that the Senator from Delaware entertains. I will call attention now to what Mr. Tupper said about it. After quoting Article XI of the treaty, he said:

That was another concession. There is no doubt at all, sir, that these were rights which under the strict terms of the treaty of 1818 they could not demand, nor could they insist upon them being granted; but at the same time I think I am within the judgment of the house on both sides when I say that in the case of a vessel which is homeward bound and requires provisions or needful supplies to take her home, if, for instance, she has some of her rigging carried away, or some of her salt washed overboard, and is obliged to lose her voyage in going back to a distant port to refit, a provision that she may obtain casual and needful supplies of that kind was demanded in the interests of good neighborhood, and it was not going too far to say that we would allow them to enjoy those advantages. Therefore, sir, I am glad to belive that Article XI will meet with the hearty approval of the house and the country, and that they will feel that we have only acted with a wise judgment, and with due regard to the best interests of Canada for the sake of removing an international unpleasantness, in putting these provisions into this treaty.

It is very clear that Mr. Tupper does not understand it as the Senator from Delaware does; it is very clear that if this treaty is ratified it opens the door for further controversy, for when the man who made it on the part of the Canadian Government gives it one construction and the Senator from Delaware, representing the Administration, gives it another, it is fair to presume that this will not cease to be a subject of controversy, but will hereafter continue to be a subject of controversy as others have been heretofore.

So there is nothing in that which has not been granted for more than fifty years to every Canadian vessel in the United States wherever she has gone.

I come now to a remarkable section as to the numbering of fishing vessels. I do not desire to spend much time upon it. I find that we are to number in a conspicuous manner every United States vessel, to have "its official number on each bow." It shall be plainly marked, be conspicuous, so that all can see it, and we shall make such regulations concerning it as we may think proper; but before they take effect we are to submit them to Her Majesty's Government; I do not know for what, whether for approval or disapproval, but the regulations can not take effect, at all events, until we have submitted them. How long is it since we have submitted questions of this kind to a foreign power? Some years ago, about 1852, when there was some trouble up on the Canadian border, an English cruiser was called upon to seize some American vessels that the Canadian authorities said were intruding and violating the provisions of the treaty, or if not the treaty, some of their local statutes, and the British officer replied, "How am I to know whether they are American vessels or not? Are they marked?" Now it is proposed that there shall be no trouble of that kind hereafter. They are to be marked. They will be marked if this treaty should become operative; but it will not.

Now I come to Article XIV, which I think is a very remarkable one. I confess, if everything else had been according to my judgment, that the reading of this article alone would render it utterly impossible for me, with my ideas of right and duty, to vote for this treaty.

ARTICLE XIV.

The penalties for unlawfully fishing in the waters, bays, creeks, and harbors, referred to in Article I of this treaty, may extend to forfeiture of the boat or vessel, and appurtenances, and also of the supplies and cargo aboard when the offense was committed; and for preparing in such waters to unlawfully fish therein, penalties shall be fixed by the court, not to exceed those for unlawfully fishing, and for any other violation of the laws of Great Britain, Canada, or Newfoundland relating to the right of fishery in such waters, bays, creeks, or harbors, penalties shall be fixed by the court, not exceeding in all $3 for every ton of the boat or vessel concerned. The boat or vessel may be holden for penalties and forfeitures.

We were told by Senators who addressed the Senate that this was a valuable provision, because we knew just the penalties to be attached; we knew just what the fishermen would suffer. When the Barbary State pirates went out from the African coast and seized a vessel that was sailing by, they confiscated the cargo and they confiscated the ship and sold the men into slavery; and there is nothing more left for the

British Government to do, unless when it gets a ship and the cargo it should propose to sell the men.

Somebody said when this was under discussion heretofore, that the men escaped with their lives. They take all a man has got; they take his ship, they take his stock in trade, his fish, and everything on the vessel. For what? For fishing in waters as to which he can not tell when he goes out without a marine-glass, and frequently can not tell with a glass, whether he is within the prohibited waters or not. No matter how he gets there, anxious as he may be to keep within the waters that are unquestionably his, to keep out of the forbidden waters, if by wind or tide he finds himself, or a Canadian official asserts that he is, within the forbidden waters, he loses his ship and he loses his cargo. He does not lose his life! What a wonderful condescension after they take all the poor devil has.

The offense of fishing in English waters wilfully and corruptly might ustify the forfeiture of the vessel; but does it justify it where it is done by mistake? There is no saving clause; there is no assertion that if he purposely goes there he shall suffer; there is no way that he can get out by pleading that he was carried in by the great tides that rise twenty-odd feet and flow with a velocity which will carry fishermen out of their soundings and beyond their reckonings; and yet if a fisherman goes in there perforce of wind and weather he is to be seized by these people who have for years shown themselves to be the deadly enemies of our fishermen, and who have declared officially that every American fisherman who came into those waters is an injury to Canadian interests, and that they intend, if they can, to deprive us of the privilege of fishing in those waters. And yet we are told that this is a treaty that the American Senate ought to ratify in this year 1888!

Mr. President, I say it is a barbarism to punish any man with forfeiture of his boat and the forfeiture of his cargo who does not go there with willful intention to violate the law, and there ought to have been a provision in this treaty that only in case of willful violation of the law should fishermen be amenable to such extreme penalties.

Then, "preparing to fish," mending his nets within the waters with intent "to unlawfully fish therein."

I do not know whether this means unlawfully fishing within the forbidden waters, but I will assume that it does for this argument. I will concede that it does.

What is "preparing to fish?" Mending his nets, getting ready his lines, fixing up his ship; and who is to determine whether he is preparing to fish in the forbidden waters, and if he is found guilty, what is the penalty? They were careful to say "for unlawful fishing."

For preparing in such waters to unlawfully fish therein, penalties shall be fixed by the court, not to exceed those for unlawfully fishing.

So for preparing to fish they may forfeit his vessel, they may forfeit his cargo, they may turn him adrift in a Canadian port to get home as best he may, and they may do it upon the testimony of the men who become the owners of one-half of his ship and one-half of his cargo; and when he is seized for preparing to fish and taken into a British port he must prove that he was not preparing to fish, and he must prove that he was not preparing to fish within the forbidden waters. The burden of proof is on him. Every fact that is necessary to establish his defense he must prove affirmatively.

The Senator from Delaware and other Senators have attempted to make it appear that this is but the usual customs law. This is not true. It is a different thing. The rule is that where a man has a license to do a certain thing and he is arrested and it is charged that he had not a license, he must produce the license, and the burden of proof is on him because the proof is supposed to be with him. But when a vessel is seized for being over the line, when it is seized for preparing to fish or unlawfully fishing, he has the burden of proof on him. Can he better produce the proof than the other party? Do we not reverse all the ordinary rules of courts and all the ordinary rules that apply to transactions between men, and put him in a hostile court away from home with the witnesses interested in securing his condemnation, and put him upon the proof? Why, sir, it is a most outrageous provision in the treaty, and I have the authority of the Secretary of State that it is an outrageous provision in the statute; I have the authority of his minister to Great Britain that it is outrageous to thus proceed.

Mr. Phelps, speaking of this very principle, said in a letter of December 2, 1886:

Mr. Phelps to Lord Iddesleigh.

LEGATION OF THE UNITED STATES, *London, December* 2, 1886,

MY LORD: Referring to the conversation I had the honor to hold with your lordship on the 30th November, relative to the request of my Government that the owners of the David J. Adams may be furnished with a copy of the original reports, stating the charges on which that vessel was seized by the Canadian authorities, I desire now to place before you in writing the grounds upon which this request is preferred.

In the suit that is now going on in the admiralty court at Halifax, for the purpose of condemning the vessel, still further charges have been added. And the Government of Canada seek to avail themselves of a clause in the act of the Canadian Parliament of May 22, 1868, which is in these words: "In case a dispute arises as to whether any seizure has or has not been legally made or as to whether the person seizing was or was not authorized to seize under this act * * * the burden of proving the illegality of the seizure shall be on the owner or claimant."

I can not quote this provision without saying that it is, in my judgment, in violation of the principles of natural justice, as well as of those of the common law. That a man should be charged by police or executive officers with the commission of an offense and then be condemned upon trial unless he can prove himself to be innocent is a proposition that is incompatible with the fundamental ideas upon which the administration of justice proceeds. But it is sought in the present case to carry the proposition much further, and to hold that the party inculpated must not only prove himself innocent of the offense on which his vessel was seized, but also of all other charges upon which it might have been seized that may be afterward brought forward and set up at the trial.

What will be the opportunity of the American fisherman to escape condemnation in a Canadian court—seizing him for one thing and compelling him to prove that he was not guilty of another? Why, Mr. President, it is a cunningly-devised scheme to confiscate the property of American citizens. It is not much better in my judgment, nay, I doubt whether it is any better, than the system by which the pirates went out and seized the vessels as they passed by. For them, at least, there was a chance for a fair fight, but there is none given to these men, either before or after. Lord Iddesleigh replied to this by saying it was the usual customs law. Mr. Phelps denied it. I quote what Lord Iddesleigh said:

With respect to the statement in your note that a clause in the Canadian act of May 22, 1868, to the effect that, "In case a dispute arises as to whether any seizure has or has not been legally made, or as to whether the person seizing was or was not authorized to seize under this act, the burden of proving the illegality of the seizure shall be on the owner or claimant," is in violation of the principles of national justice, as well as those of the common law, I have to observe that the statutes referred to is cap. 61 of 1868, which provides for the issue of licenses to foreign fishing vessels, and for the forfeiture of such vessels fishing without a license; and that the provisions of Article X, to which you take exception, are commonly found in laws against smuggling, and are based on the rule of law that a man who pleads that he holds a license or other simllar document shall be put to the proof of his plea and required to produce the document,

I beg leave to add that the provisions of that statute, so far as they relate to the issue of licenses, has been in operation since the year 1870.

I have, etc.,

IDDESLEIGH.

To this Mr. Phelps replied:

It is in the act to which the one above referred to is an amendment that is found the provision to which I drew attention in a note to Lord Iddesleigh of December 2, 1886, by which it is enacted that in case a dispute arises as to whether any seizure has or has not been legally made, the burden of proving the illegality of the seizure shall be upon the owner or claimant.

In his reply to that note of January 11, 1887, his lordship intimates that this provision is intended only to impose upon a person claiming a license the burden of proving it. But a reference to the act shows that such is by no means the restriction of the enactment. It refers in the broadest and clearest terms to any seizure that is made under the provisions of the act, which covers the whole subject of protection against illegal fishing; and it applies not only to the proof of a license to fish, but to all questions of fact whatever, necessary to a determination as to the legality of a seizure or the authority of the person making it.

There is no mistaking what this act means. It is not in accordance with our acts. We have nothing of that kind on our statute-books. Mr. Bayard's attention was called to it, and in a letter to Mr. Phelps, of January 27, 1887, Mr. Bayard said:

Mr. Bayard to Mr. Phelps.

DEPARTMENT OF STATE, *Washington, January 27, 1887.*

SIR: Your dispatch No. 416, of the 12th instant, transmitting a copy of the note dated the 11th, received by you from the late Lord Iddesleigh, in response to your note of December 2, 1886, requesting copies of the papers in the case of the David J. Adams, has been received.

* * * * * *

The concluding part of Lord Iddesleigh's note seems to demand attention, inasmuch as the argument employed to justify the provisions of article 10 of the Canadian Statutes, cap. 61 of 1868, which throw on the claimant the burden of proving the illegality of a seizure, appears to rest upon the continued operation of article 1 of that statute, relative to the issue of licenses to foreign fishing vessels. The note in question states "that the provisions of that statute, so far as they relate to the issues of licenses, has [have ?] been in operation since the year 1870."

It appears from the correspondence exchanged in 1870 between this Department and Her Majesty's minister in Washington (see the volume of Foreign Relations, 1870, pages 407-411) that on the 8th of January, 1870, an order in council of the Canadian Government decreed "that the system of granting fishing license to foreign vessels under the act 31 Vic., cap. 61, be discontinued, and that henceforth all foreign fishermen be prevented from fishing in the waters of Canada."

During the continuance of the fishery articles of the treaty of Washington Canadian fishing licenses were not required for fishermen of the United States, and since the termination of those articles, July 1, 1885, this Department has not been advised of the resumption of the licensing system under the statute aforesaid.

This is an old statute. I desire to call attention to what has been said about it heretofore. It does not seem necessary that anybody should be cited as authority on a question of that kind. It does seem to me that every fair-minded man will see that the law is an odious law, that it is liable to great abuse, and to bring our fishermen within that law is to expose them to great disaster. I have here Mr. Forsyth's letter to Lord Aberdeen commenting on this, and I will read it from Sabine's Report on Fisheries, because it is the handiest book to read. He says:

Well did Mr. Forsyth say that some of its provisions were "violations of well-established principles of the common law of England and of the principles of all just powers and all civilized nations, and seemed to be expressly designed to enable Her Majesty's authorities with perfect impunity to seize and confiscate American vessels, and to embezzle, almost indiscriminately, the property of our citizens employed in the fisheries on the coast of the British possessions." Well, too, did Mr. Everett stigmatize it as possessing "none of the qualities of the law of civilized states but its forms;" and Mr. Davis, as being "a law of shameful character," and "evidently designed to legalize marauding upon an industrious, enterprising class of men, who have no means to contend with such sharp and unwarrantable weapons of warfare."

So, Mr. President, the provision that they shall take nothing from these people who are guilty of unlawful fishing, and those who are preparing to fish, etc., but their fishing vessels and cargoes, is, under the circumstances the way the law is administered, an extremely harsh provision. But they were not satisfied with that, and further penalties are provided:

And for any other violation of the laws of Great Britain, Canada, or Newfoundland relating to the right of fishery in such waters, bays, creeks, or harbors, penalties shall be fixed by the court, not exceeding in all $3 for every ton of the boat or vessel concerned. The boat or vessel may be holden for such penalties and forfeitures.

This is the first time that the United States has anywhere recognized the right of the Canadian authorities to legislate in such a way as to interfere with the rights of American fishermen under the treaty of 1818. We have asserted over and over again that all this legislation was without authority of law, that we would not submit to have the Canadian authorities providing what we might do or what we might not do, except so far as provided for in treaty; and it is a notable fact that Great Britain never ratified or approved any acts of this character until 1886—until within the history of this present Administration.

When this Administration came into power they were not attempting and did not dare to attempt to enforce these Canadian laws. It was out of an attempt to enforce these Canadian laws as to fishing on Sunday that the controversy arose in which the Secretary of State, Mr. Evarts, compelled a payment by the British Government. Now we have agreed in this treaty, if it becomes the law, that every petty British North American province and Canada and Great Britain can pass any law upon the subject of fishing that they see fit, and we are bound by it. They fix the size of the meshes of the seine; they fix when it may be thrown and when it may be drawn; they tell us that we can not fish on Sunday or on the Queen's holidays, or any other time; and for the violation of such laws the American fishermen is liable to punishment in a Canadian court, administered, as I said before, by a hostile people.

They may fish, as it is suggested, in the open seas, as they have done, to which we have paid no attention so far; but our men are liable to be punished for violations of this kind of legislation, which we shall be estopped from complaining of, because we here say they have a right to made it if they see fit, and we reserve to ourselves no right of criticism. They may be taken into a Canadian court where they can be fined $3 per ton on their vessel, and a vessel of 100 tons could be fined $300, and how often may that be repeated? As often as any officious Canada official, moved by his desire to get part of the plunder that shall be taken from these fishermen, institutes a prosecution in the Canadian courts.

It is true they have provided in this treaty that "the proceedings shall be summary and as inexpensive as practicable." But what of that? It may be of some advantage to a poor fisherman who is to be ruined to know how quickly he is to be ruined. It may be also of some advantage to his Canadian opponent to put him through the court on quick time, that he may try him again, because he can be picked up for all sorts of complaints. I think there is quite as much for Canada in that as there is for us, so far as the prompt proceedings are concerned.

Is there anybody living who has studied this question and who knows the temper of the Canadians, who knows the difficulties surrounding the fishermen, who does not know that where there has heretofore been one case of conflict between the Canadians and our fishermen there will be a hundred such conflicts under this treaty? Does not everybody know that we are opening the door for continued agitation and continued trouble?

It must be evident to everybody that when we surrender to the British Government thé right to fix the season in which we may fish, the methods by which we may fish, the character of the fish that we may put in our barrels, and all this, we have subjected our people to such a condition of things as renders fishing absolutely worthless, and I do not hesitate to say here that, in my judgment—and I believe in the judgment of men better qualified to judge than I—that in two years they will make it impossible for American fishermen under this treaty to fish in waters where our rights are as unquestioned as they are in the Delaware Bay.

There is one other provision in the treaty of which I will not speak at length, and that is Article XV. That is where we agree to buy commercial privileges at an expense, Mr. Tupper says, of about $1,800,000 a year.

Mr. FRYE.   Limited commericial privileges.

Mr. TELLER.   Limited commercial privileges, commercial privileges which I insist Canadian vessels have had for fifty years everywhere in our ports, unless it may be in some few of the South Atlantic ports, and I do not believe they have ever been disturbed in them there, but on all the New England coast and in all the great harbors of this country they can go and do what we propose to pay to the British Government $1,800,000 a year for, in the removal of import duties.

The fifteenth article is what they started out for when they began this negotiation.   Mr. Tupper declared that he came here, and he supposed that what they were to do was to get up a reciprocity treaty, and he cites Mr. Bayard's letter in proof of it, and nobody can doubt it. I do not know that anybody disputes it.   So there is a combination, a union, between the Democratic party and the British party to secure to them legislation through this fisheries excitement that they could not hope and could not expect otherwise to obtain.

I will not go through with this matter in detail.   The Senator from Massachusetts [Mr. HOAR] touched it with great power and presented it in a way that it seemed to me ought to have made every American blush for his Government.   One thing is certain, Mr. President.   The masterly way in which he presented it caused the Secretary of State, usually calm and collected, to forget the high position which he occupies. and induced him to submit himself to a newspaper interview, wherein he speaks of the speech made by the Senator from Massachusetts in terms more consistent with a fish-market than with a diplomatic position, and in that same interview he takes occasion to say that the Republican members of the American Senate are not honest, that we are not truthful when we say that we do not regard this as a proper treaty, that we are moved simply by our hatred of the Democratic Administration, and then he slaps himself on the chest and declares that he is above partisanship, and he only of all people is above such small and wicked things.

Mr. President, if there is a disgraceful chapter in American history

It is in connection with this negotiation, by which it is undertaken by the Secretary of State to aid and assist the Democratic party by allying it with the Canadian party and the British party. It is fortunate for us that in a hundred years no such exhibition has been made heretofore, and it is to be hoped that it will not occur again. It was not intended that it should be known; there was nothing said about it, and if Mr. Tupper had not, in his innocence, mentioned the subject in the Canadian Parliament, I suppose it would have escaped observation except in a general way. Those who believed this treaty was a surrender of American rights without equivalents might have believed that there were some reasons for it, I do not know what; I am unable to state.

I know that here is a treaty made by the present Administration which, if it had remained of the opinion that it was all through the year 1886 and through a good portion of the year 1887, it would not have sent to the Senate. I do not know what influences were brought to bear. I do not know whether it was supposed it would be popular with Great Britain and Canada and whether it would or would not assist in the coming election. I know that it is a treaty unfit to be made, and the transaction is one for which the Department and the whole country, so far as it has had any connection with it, ought to be ashamed.

Mr. Tupper told us that this was but the beginning, in substance that they could not carry this load all at once, but we were coming to the question of free fish and free intercourse between the United States and Great Britain.

The President told us in his message that he did not think it was worth while to pass upon that question in the treaty, but to make it contingent. Why, sir, the President of the United States knew that he could not modify or change the impost duty laws. He knew that the duty on fish was part of the law of the land. The Democratic House of Representatives referred that matter in the Forthy-eighth Congress to its Judiciary Committee, and its Judiciary Committee with one accord, without exception, both political parties concurring, reported that it was not in the power of the executive department to negotiate a treaty that should amend, modify, or change the import laws. But there was an understanding that the Democratic party should work in the House for this purpose, and they did so work.

I desire to submit some portions of Mr. Tupper's remarks upon this question, which have already been read in part, and, therefore, I will ask to put them in without reading:

Sir CHARLES TUPPER. I do not intend to insult both the great political parties of this country who have since 1854 and long before maintained that the interests of Canada—the interests of British North America—were intimately bound up in obtaining free intercourse with the United States for our natural products—I do not intend to insult the two great parties in this country by telling them that they were fools, that they did not know what they were doing. Down to the present hour we have adopted the policy on both sides of the House, and we have pledged ourselves to the people to do everything that lay in our power to obtain a free market for the natural products of our country with the United State, and I say you must answer me the question as to whether that was an act of supreme folly, or whether it was wise statesmanship on the part of both parties in this country to adopt that policy, before you ask me such a question as " who pays the duty?"

I say that under this bill which has been introduced and which I believe will pass, for it does not require two-thirds of the Senate, where the Republican majority is only one in the whole House, to pass the bill, it requires a majority of one only, and I am very sanguine that this bill will pass during the present session. Modified it may be, but I am inclined to think the amendments will be still more in the interests of Canada than as the bill stands to-day. If this is the case I think we may congratulate ourselves upon securing the free admission of our lumber, upon which was paid during the last year no less than $1,315,-450. On copper-ore, made free by the Mills bill, we paid, or there was paid—to

make it meet the views of the honorable gentlemen of posite more correctly—
$96,945. On salt, $21,992 duty was paid. This is rendered free by the Mills bill.
I am sorry to find, as I hoped would be the case, from the first copy of the bill
that came to me, that potatoes were not included amongst vegetables. I am
sorry to find there is a doubt as to whether the term "vegetables not specially
enumerated" will not exclude potatoes.

In grappling with this policy of making the natural products of the two countries free, you do not expect any person who wants to carry a bill to put a heav-
ier load upon his shoulders than he is able to carry, lest he may break down
and do nothing. You expect him to take it in detail, and, as I believe, you will
find the policy contained in this bill of making those natural products of Canada free, carried out until you have perfect freedom of intercourse between the
natural products of Canada and the United States of America. Of wool we sent
last year 1,319,309 pounds of one kind and a variety of other kinds, upon which
a duty was paid to the extent of $183,852. Now, as I say on articles of prime im-
portance and interest to Canada the removal of duty by the Mills bill amounts
to no less than $1,800,193. You will be glad to hear that I do not intend to de-
tain the house any longer. In discharge of the duties—the very onerous and
important duties—of one of Her Majesty's plenipotentiaries at that conference,
I have steadily kept in view what, in my heart and judgment, I believed were
the best interests of Canada. In the measure which I have the honor to submit
to this house I believe will be found embodied a bill which it is of the most
vital importance to Canada to pass.

As it stands to-day the Government of the United States have only my signature to sustain the course that has been taken. I was not there as the representative of the Government of Canada, nor can my signature to the treaty neces-
sarily imply the approval and support of even the Government of Canada. I
occupied on that occasion the position of one of Her Majesty's plenipotentiaries,
charged not only with the responsibility of what I owed to Canada, but also
the responsibility of my duty to the empire. I can only say, sir, that I felt I
would best discharge my duty to the empire by steadily keeping in view the
interest of Canada. I believe, sir, that there is no way in which any public
man in this country can promote the interests of the great empire of which
we form a part, better, or as well, as by taking such a course of public action
as will build up a great British community on this northern portion of the continent of America.

I believe, sir, that we owe it to the empire as well as to ourselves steadily
to keep in view every measure that will conduce to the rapid progress of Canada, the development of our inexhaustible resources, and the building up of a
great and powerful British dominion on this side of the Atlantic. I say, sir,
that in the discharge of my duty I have steadily kept that conviction in view,
and I believe the course which has been pursued will not only commend itself
to the judgment and the support of the great majority in this house, but that
the great majority of the people in this country will feel that in the adoption of
this treaty we are taking a step that is calculated to conduce to the progress
and greatness and best interests of Canada.

Mr. Tupper tells us that the whole Democratic party of the United
States is in sympathy and accord with this view. It would look very
much as if that was the fact. Democrats on this floor who last year
took the position that there was no necessity for any further legislation, that there was no necessity for any further treaty, are now up-
braiding us because we do not see the necessity of this treaty. They
upbraid us because we do not approve of the provisions of this treaty.
The Secretary of State, who had declared through his minister that it
was not a question of a new treaty, but a question of the construction
of the present treaty, says that it is a valuable treaty and one that ought
to be ratified by the Senate.

I denied before that it was a construction of the treaty of 1818 and I
declared then that it was a new treaty. I desire to read just a few words
from a letter of Mr. Trescott, a prominent Democrat, upon that point.
Mr. Trescott is well known in this country as an able diplomat, and
passing upon this question he says:

There is not in this treaty an article, a phrase, a word, which recognizes our
construction. It is absolutely rejected. The consequence is that this is a new
treaty, not a construction of an old one. Whatever it may do for the future, it
can not help the past, and thus the position taken by the country through Congress as to our reciprocal commercial rights and the protests by Mr. Bayard
against those rights can find no support in any of its provisions, and our claims
for compensation must either be abandoned or we must begin over again the

angry and useless reclamations of the last two or three years. It is indeed a very curious fact that, although the necessity for any treaty sprang from the violent, persistent, and annoying seizures by the Canadian and Newfoundland authorities, there is not in the whole treaty a reference to these seizures or a suggestion of any right to or any method of compensation.

Mr. President, I have alluded to an interview of the Secretary of State. This interview purports to have been on the 11th of July of this year. I would not willingly do injustice to the Secretary of State, and I would not assume that any newspaper article expressed his views if there were not good reasons to suppose that such was the fact; but this publication in the Sun, of the city of Baltimore, has been before the country for some time, and I am not aware that the Secretary has ever in any manner indicated his disapproval of the sentiments put in his mouth and said to have been uttered by him.

The editor of this paper proceeds, before he reaches the interview, to castigate the Senate, undoubtedly upon information furnished him by the Secretary of State, and then he reaches a point where he says the Secretary was interviewed and made "the following statement." It is too long to read, and I propose, unless there is objection, to put the whole interview, including the comments of the newspaper, in my speech. I propose, if this article is not true, to put it in official form so that the Secretary of State may, if he desires, contradict it. He may think it beneath his dignity to deny a newspaper report, but it is a report so unjust to him if untrue, and so unjust to the Senate if true, that I do not think he can afford to overlook it. Therefore I will insert it in the RECORD:

THE FISHERIES DISCUSSION—MR. BAYARD REPLIES TO SENATOR HOAR—THE ADMINISTRATION JEALOUS OF THE RIGHTS OF AMERICAN SEAMEN, AND HAS MAINTAINED THEM.

[Special dispatch to the Baltimore Sun.]

WASHINGTON, July 11.

The elaborate production with which Mr. HOAR occupied the Senate yesterday afternoon bears the marks of most careful preparation. It is undeniably able and ingenious, although anything but ingenuous. It will be used as a campaign document, as will various of the speeches of other Republican Senators on the fisheries treaty. The crusade against the treaty inaugurated on the Republican side of the Senate is palpably dishonest. The evidences are thick that had it been negotiated by a Republican administration it would have been defended as solidly by them as it is now denounced.

Unbiased public sentiment in New England, according to all reliable reports, steadily tends to approve of its provisions. But with the desire and hope of making political capital and preventing a Democratic Administration from having the honor of reconciling international differences, which at one time threatened to lead to such serious results, the Senate Republicans have deliberately addressed themselves to the task of falsifying facts, perverting argument, and obstructing a settlement which they know in their hearts abates not one jot or tittle of American rights and American honor. If they were sincere in their denunciation of the treaty they would reject it outright, as they have the full power to do. To the contrary, the programme is said to be to exhaust all the vocabulary of vituperation and misrepresentation upon it, to be used as campaign literature, and then postpone its further consideration until December next. Should the Senate reject the treaty, there are good grounds for belief that the President would immediately put into execution the provisions of the retaliation act.

Although so much stress has been laid upon this act and the failure of the Executive to avail of it by Republican Senators and members from New England, it is the very last thing they want him to do, for it would injure New England ten times more than it would Canada. In all probability Senators FRYE and HOAR would be among the first to rush to the White House and beseech the President to withdraw his proclamation. A very striking illustration of honest sentiment in New England on the subject of the treaty is found in the action of the Democrats of Maine. Their nominee for governor is Mr. Putnam, one of the commissioners who negotiated it, and their platform indorses the treaty in

TELLER——4

length and breadth, without qualification or amendment. Mr. Putnam is making one of the most lively and animated canvasses that has ever occurred in the State of Maine, and wherever he speaks he makes the treaty a distinct issue. He writes here that there have never been larger or more enthusiastic meetings in the State.

Other Maine Democrats send word here that the Republican majority will be materially cut down, if not entirely wiped out. Perhaps these predictions may be regarded as too sanguine, but the fact of big Democratic meetings and intense public enthusiasm is quite sufficient proof that there is not a universal desire in Maine to crucify Cleveland and Bayard for surrendering everything to Canada, as Senator Frye wants us to believe. Senator Hoar's remarkable mis-statement of facts will, of course, be replied to in due time by Senators on the other side. He seemed to take especial pleasure in attacking and misrepresenting the action of Secretary Bayard. In view of the important questions involved and the public interest the comments of the Secretary on Mr. Hoar's speech will be eagerly read. In conversation with your correspondent on the subject to-day Mr. Bayard said:

"It is hardly worth the trouble to deny the utterances of men who willfully pervert the truth to suit their own purposes.

"The remarks of Senator Hoar are disengenuous in the extreme; the speech is a hysterical scream from beginning to end. His statements are most untrue, most unfair. He makes charges which he must know to be without foundation, as the full records concerning them are in the archives of the Senate in the form of executive documents. His discourse is more barren of fairness and honesty than any document I have known, which consumed three weeks in the preparation, and supposed to be the result of research for the truth only. It is not to be wondered that we failed to consult with the New England Senators as to the nature of the negotiations with the British and Canadian protocolists. We hardly seek roses where thorns only abide, nor do we go to enemies for friendly advice. Mr. Ingalls on one occasion asked whether it should be blood or negotiation. Mr. Edmunds replied, 'Neither.' These men were sworn to defeat any attempt to settle existing difficulty. Evidently their purpose was, and is, to embarrass the Administration. Was it to such men that we should turn for friendly counsel?

"Mr. Hoar avers that this Department declined to furnish the Senate, in response to resolution calling therefor, the proposal and counter proposals made while the joint commission was in session. This is absolutely untrue. As is usual in such cases it was agreed that the proceedings of the commission should be regarded as of a strictly confidential nature. The meetings were to be of a purely informal character, and when it was deemed advisable to publish any of the conclusions reached or proposals made, it was not to be done until the written statement had been signed by all the protocolists. I have already answered this charge. My statement is printed in Executive Document 127, published by the Senate March 26, 1888, it being an answer to a Senate resolution calling for the transmission of copies of the minutes and daily protocols of the meeting of the commissioners who negotiated the treaty with Great Britain.

"In that letter I stated: 'In conformity with the invariable course pursued in previous negotiations when the conference met it was agreed that an honorable confidence should be maintained in its deliberations, and that only results should be announced, and such other matters as the joint protocolists should sign under the direction of the plenipotentiaries. With this understanding, which was strictly kept, the discussions of the conference proceeded, through its numerous and prolonged sessions, with that freedo · and uniformity in the exchange of views which the nature of the negotiation required, and without which its progress would have been materially hampered and any agreement rendered very difficult of attainment. No stenographer was employed, and no minutes or daily protocols were agreed upon and signed by the joint protocolists other than those already transmitted to the Senate.

"'Upon the conclusion of the treaty some members of the conference at once left the city under the pressure of other duties, and it is thus probable that some statements were excluded that otherwise might have been placed in the joint protocols. After the conference had finally adjourned and Sir Charles Tupper had returned to Ottawa a request was received through the British minister that assent be given to the publication of a certain proposal which had been submitted by the British plenipotentiaries and declined by the American. I inclose a copy of the papers referred to, and they were printed in the executive document. These were at the disposal of Senator Hoar, and prove his charge to have been utterly unfounded. I will explain to you the reasons which led me to grant the permission to print the proposal made by Sir Charles Tupper, which is as follows:

"'That with the view of removing all causes of difference in connection with the fisheries it is proposed by Her Majesty's plenipotentiaries that the fishermen of both countries shall have all the privileges enjoyed during the existence of the fisheries articles of the Washington treaty, in consideration of a mutual arrangement providing for greater freedom of commercial intercourse between the United States and Canada and Newfoundland.'

" This proposition was declined because it necessitated an adjustment of the present tariff of the United States by Congressional action, which adjustment was considered to be manifestly impracticable of accomplishment through the form of treaty under the circumstances then existing.

" Sir Charles Tupper was greatly interested in the acceptance of this proposal, which had for its object the abolishment of the duty on fish and fish oil. His government greatly desired that an arrangement to this end should be made. Therefore, when Sir Charles Tupper returned home, he was confronted with the demand, ' Where is the free fish and free fish oil you promised to obtain for us? ' 'I did not succeed,' he was obliged to answer, 'but I made the effort.' To prove that he had endeavored to accomplish that which the people so greatly desired he asked for permission to print his proposal and our declination. It was but fair to grant the request, and it was granted. These facts were known to Mr. Hoar, or could have been learned with no trouble whatever.

" It is true that I made no attempt to secure the right to fish in the jurisdictional waters of Canada. To obtain this concession it was required that we accede to the demand of the Canadian Government that its fish and fish oil be allowed to enter into our ports free of duty. I for one did not propose to accede to any demand. We determined to obtain our rights, nothing more, and it has cost the United States nothing to do so. What a contrast to the result of the Halifax commission which met in 1871, and of which Senator Hoar's brother was a member. On that occasion the American protocolists paid for the privilege of fishing within the 3-mile limit for twelve years $5,000,000 and abolished the duty on fish and fish-oil. Previous to the meeting of the commission a British fleet had seized a number of American vessels, but no redress was obtained or even demanded. The ratification of this treaty was agreed upon by a Republican Senate. The charming consistency of Senator Hoar is here apparent. While at one time he favored free fish and free oil, when he learned that negotiations were to be entered into concerning the fisheries he introduced the following resolution in the Senate, February 24, 1887:

" ' Resolved, That it is the judgment of the Senate that under present circumstances no negotiation should be under taken with Great Britain in regard to existing difficulties with her province of Canada which has for its object the reduction, change, or abolition of any of our existing duties on imports.'

" Now the Senator censures the Department for failing to obtain the concession, which he knew depended upon the abolition of the duty on fish and fish oil. It was a most impudent resolution, as well as inconsistent, for the President was at liberty to enter into any negotiation he saw fit. As a matter of fact, no sane man would give $50,000 a year for the privilege of fishing within the 3-mile limit, notwithstanding the enormous sum paid for the concession by the commission of 1871. I did not consult with the New England Senators, but I did hear the opinions on this point of men known to be thoroughly conversant with the subject. Professor Baird told me that the men I had here in connection with the 3-mile limit question knew more about the fishery question than any one else in New England. They told me the privilege was valueless. Moreover, there is a report which Mr. Hoar might have read coming from a committee of Republican Senators, which also avows the privilege to be of no value. I therefore had the best of information and advice as to the worth of the concession which once cost $5,000,000.

" It is not true that the State Department does not press claims for damages. The case referred to by Mr. Hoar is that which was covered by the following paragraph of my letter to the Senate published in Executive Document No. 127, March 26, 1888: ' Every point submitted to the conference is covered by the paper now in possession of the Senate, excepting the question of damages sustained by our fishermen, which, being met by the counter claim for damages to British vessels in Bering Sea, was left for future settlement.' This was determined the best course that could be pursued by the commission. As their claim exceeded ours I was very willing to agree to this. Senator Hoar also refers to the case of the Bridgewater. Within two days after the case was reported to this Department the claim for damages presented by the owners of the vessel was on its way to England.

" The British Government is now investigating the case. Again he charges that I allowed the flag of an American vessel to be hauled down by the officers of a British cruiser. For that act this country received a full apology from England. As much can not be said when indignities were heaped upon American seamen in years gone by. The Administration is jealous of the rights of American seamen and has maintained them. There was more trouble of this character during General Grant's administrations than there has been in Mr. Cleveland's.

" No provision was inserted in the treaty to prevent the ordering off of American vessels from the jurisdictional waters of Canada, because the surrendering of the headland right by the British plenipotentiaries rendered such provision unnecessary. Imagine a line drawn from one headland of Prince Edward's

Island to the other. It would be about 100 miles long. It would inclose at the farthest point from shore about 30 miles of water. Under the old rights the Canadian Government could order beyond that line any American vessel that happened to get within it. This right has been surrendered. For this reason it was not necessary to provide against the ordering off of vessels.

"Senator HOAR did not read Sir Charles Tupper's statement with the proper knowledge of the meaning of English words or he would not have made the rash statement that that gentleman said I made promises for the President, House of Representatives, and Democratic party as to what would be done for Great Britain and Canada. Sir Charles's speech contains no such statement. I did tell Sir Charles Tupper that when Canada treated American citizens fairly he might then expect some steps looking to the establishment of more friendly relations between the two countries.

"For my own part I favor reciprocity with Canada. The existing conditions are absurd. We pay Canada for our coal and we pay her for hers. A duty is paid us on Canadian fish and we have to pay Canada a duty on our fish. It is manifestly wrong. Reciprocity has been favored by such men as Webster, Marcy, Everett, Arthur, Frelinghuysen, and many others. Some of the Republicans go so far as to favor commercial union.

"There is one statement I wish to make particularly emphatic, and that is, the American fishermen have under the treaty every right of value to them, and the Government has been put to no expense thereby. Their interests will be guarded and no attempt to deprive them of their rights tolerated. It is my hope that all trouble will be ended by the establishment of full reciprocity between Canada and the United States. I had hoped, as a step toward this end, free fish and free oil would have been one of the provisions of the Mills bill, and trust that it may yet be inserted."—*Baltimore Sun*, July 12, 1888.

The Senator from New Hampshire [Mr. CHANDLER] the other day introduced in the Senate a letter from Hon. Charles Levi Woodbury concerning this matter, which is such high authority on this subject that I am inclined to add it also to the letters that appear upon this question. The Senator from New Hampshire explained to the Senate and to the country who Charles Levi Woodbury was and who he is. I suppose there are few men in the country, if there are any, who are as well qualified to speak on this subject as Mr. Woodbury; probably no one unless it be Mr. Trescott, who is also a Democratic diplomat and who has spoken in the same general direction that Mr. Woodbury has. So when Mr. Tupper says the entire Democratic party of the country are in accord with the ideas of this treaty he is mistaken. That is not the fact.

The letter of Mr. Woodbury is as follows:

To the Editor of the Sun:

SIR: The Chamberlain treaty is now before the Senate. It surrenders everything the United States have contended for since 1838, when the dispute on the 3-mile limit began, contentions which the British authorities have assented to or temporized about as often as pressed, so that really in no entire year since then have they insisted on enforcing their headland theory.

The commercial rights of the United States under the agreements of 1830 were utterly abandoned by Mr. Bayard after much previous insistence on their obligation.

The rights of common humanity toward our vessels in distress, accorded everywhere except on the Canadian coast, are hereafter to be allowed only upon the condition that the United States shall change its present registry laws by repealing them, and enacting such new ones as are acceptable to the British Government before going into effect. This of course leaves the humanity of Canada to vessels of the United States in distress withheld until the United States shall pay the consideration by repealing its laws and making such new ones.

Commercial intercourse by our fishing vessels is disallowed, but they may be permitted to buy a narrow line of supplies, whose extent would not exceed $50,000 a year, when the United States shall have repealed existing duties, now over $611,000 a year, on Canadian fish and oil, and made them free in our markets.

This is the substance of the treaty, all losses to the United States both in honor and profit. General Jackson and Mr. McLane, Van Buren and Forsyth, Stevenson and Everett, Webster, Rush, Grant, Evarts, and even Bayard and Phelps, for two of their official years, are buried beneath this treaty and their memories dishonored by its retreat from their patriotic contentions for American rights.

Cavllers have said the treaty of 1818 was wrung from our weakness, but this treaty, made in the hour of our strength, surrenders what that never did—our markets; and it doubles the waters from which it requires we shall be forever excluded.

The consequence of adopting this treaty would be the destruction of the fishery under the American flag, the paralysis of our hope of naval power, and a British monopoly of our markets, aggrandizing its dangerous naval power. Let the treaty be rejected.

CHARLES LEVI WOODBURY.

Boston, *May* 4, 1888.

Mr. President, there are some provisions of this treaty the details of which I should like to have gone into more extensively, and there are several things in connection with the history of the transactions of early times that I should like to refer to if I had not already detained the Senate to an unusual length on this subject. Suffice it to say that it is one that the American people have interest in; it is one that the American people do not consider a local question; it is one, as was said by more than one member of the House of Representatives in 1887, that does not concern a few fish. It is not a local controversy, said they; it is not a skirmish about fish, said two members at least, one of whom is now an honored member of this body; it is not a question of property, but a question of honor, of dignity, and of right. and a question whether we are to surrender for the purpose of escaping a threat of war or to escape evils of any other kind.

Mr. President, we were told here and we have been told elsewhere, that the President of the United States would put in force the act of 1887; that he would put it in force in such a way, we have been told in substance, as to disturb and destroy the business of the country; that we had armed him with a power which was very dangerous. Why, sir, if the President of the United States chooses to disturb business for the purpose of compelling decent treatment to our seamen on the northern seas, very well, let him do it.

If any other method can be devised by which the seamen may be protected in their rights, let him put us in a position of complete non-commercial intercourse, and the people of the United States will not complain. If the exclusion of fresh fish from Canada will do it, the people will not justify him in going beyond that. He can not by way of punishment to the Senate disturb the business of the country, and the Senate will not be influenced by any suggestions of newspapers, whether they get their ideas from the Secretary of State, as the Baltimore Sun seems to have done, or from anywhere else, that the business of the country is to be disturbed if we do not accept this treaty.

The Senator from Mississippi [Mr. GEORGE] said it is foredoomed to defeat. Undoubtedly, and it is foredoomed to defeat at this session, I want to say to the Senator; and if the President of the United States declines to put in force in any proper manner the statute that we enacted for that purpose, he must take the responsibility if disturbances arise, and not we. We can not be moved by threats of disturbed business any more than we can by the suggestion made by the Senator from Alabama [Mr. MORGAN] that this might lead to war, that commercial war was close on to real war. When the act of 1887 was before the Senate, the Senator from Alabama said it does not mean war, it means peace. Now, we are told that it may mean war. Who has the right to threaten the American Senate with war? Who makes war? Certainly nobody in the Senate individually and nobody in the executive department is likely to make war. Great Britain is not likely to go to war with us for that which she has absolutely abandoned and surrendered and for that which she has never vigorously enforced at any time in the history of this claim by the Canadian authorities.

Great Britain does not go to war without cause, unless she knows that she has it in her power to acquire great good to herself by so doing. It is simply absurd to talk about a war with Great Britain; it is folly. But we are as ready for war as Great Britain. We may not have as many guns, but we would have means for maintaining the honor and the dignity of the American people in a war with Great Britain or with any other country, and we will not surrender one jot or one tittle of that which belongs to us for fear of war, nor under covert threats that if we do not accept this treaty something will follow it that will be worse and the business of the country will be disturbed. We can say for ourselves on this side of the Chamber that we approach this question with as much patriotism as Senators on the other side, and we can point to the fact that until recently the legislative department of the Government and the executive department of the Government were in perfect harmony with us upon this question.